Lawrence Halprin: Changing Places

Lawrence Halprin: Changing Places

San Francisco Museum of Modern Art

3 July – 24 August 1986

Foreword by Henry T. Hopkins

Introduction by Helene Fried

Essays by Jim Burns,

Douglas Davis,

Dr. Joseph Henderson,

Teddy Kollek,

Robert F. Maguire III,

Charles Moore, and

Phyllis Tuchman

Front cover:
Drawing by Lawrence Halprin, from his notebook, 1965, ink and watercolor, 8½ x 11″. Executed in Stockholm, Sweden, with Dancers' Workshop performance of "Parades and Changes."

Back cover:
Lawrence Halprin at The Sea Ranch, 1985.
Photo by Ernest Braun.

This book was published in conjunction with the exhibition *Lawrence Halprin: Changing Places* on view at the San Francisco Museum of Modern Art from 3 July to 24 August 1986.

© 1986 by the San Francisco Museum of Modern Art, 401 Van Ness Avenue, San Francisco, California 94102-4582.

The San Francisco Museum of Modern Art is supported in part by the California Arts Council, the Institute of Museum Services, the National Endowment for the Arts, the San Francisco Foundation, and the San Francisco Hotel Tax Fund.

Library of Congress Cataloging in Publication Data

Halprin, Lawrence.
    Lawrence Halprin: changing places: [exhibition]
San Franciso Museum of Modern Art.

    Bibliography: p.
    1. Halprin, Lawrence — Exhibitions.   2. Landscape architects — United States — Biography — Exhibitions.
3. City planners — United States — Biography — Exhibitions.   4. Landscape architecture — Exhibitions.
5. City planning — Exhibitions.   6. San Francisco Museum of Modern Art — Exhibitions.   I. Burns, Jim, 1926-   II. San Francisco Museum of Modern Art.
III. Title.
SB470.H35H35   1986   720′.92′4   86-10158
ISBN 0-918471-06-0

Designer: Suzanne Anderson-Carey
Editor: Lynne Creighton Neall
Typesetter: Type City, San Francisco
Printer: Balding & Mansell, Great Britain

Contents

Acknowledgments

I started my own office in 1949. At the beginning, my commissions were largely for private gardens and backyards. They were fun to do and I hoped to apply their lessons to the larger world of cities and regions. Gradually the larger projects arrived and with them the office expanded. It was a time of intense excitement and explorations into areas for which none of us in those days had experience or training. So, we trained ourselves in town planning and transportation systems; in the mini-architecture for shelters, kiosks, shopping areas, and playgrounds; in street-furniture design and graphics. As the office expanded it reached out into what seemed vital to new approaches in conserving the environment: into ecology and urban conservation, as well as urban design and methods of encouraging citizen's participation through Taking Part workshops.

At each stage of our development, new people joined our group. Their input and creative energies were vital to our processes. I would like to acknowledge each and every one of them in celebration of all the passion they brought to our explorations.

Among these many people, special acknowledgment should be made to Dean Abbott, Don Carter, Jim Coleman, Angela Danadjieva, Sue Yung Li Ikeda, Charles Moore, Sat Nishita, Richard Reynolds, Richard Vignolo, and Jean Walton. Of these, certain people need to be acknowledged for their specific contributions. These include: Charles Moore and William Turnbull for Lovejoy Plaza; Angela Danadjieva for Ira Keller Fountain and Seattle Freeway Park; Richard Reynolds and Don Carter for Sea Ranch; Jim Burns for workshopping; and Sue Yung Li Ikeda, my partner for the RoundHouse projects.

Our present group consists of an unusual combination of staff and close associates among whom are Dee Mullen, Dai Williams, Mary Jo Deicke, Jeri Sulley, Mendy Lowe, Michael O'Leary, David Fischer, Jim Burns, Willie Lang, Paul Scardina, Peter McCormick, Doug and Regula Campbell, and Shlomo Aronson.

No mention can adequately acknowledge the special involvement of Anna Halprin's profound contribution to my creative life, particularly to our mutually developed concepts of scoring, environmental choreography, and my involvement in workshops as a generator of creativity and a process of education.

Lawrence Halprin

Foreword

The presentation of this exhibition, dealing with important projects drawn from the design, landscape, and architectural worlds of Lawrence Halprin, is a true indication of the role of the newly established Department of Architecture and Design at the San Francisco Museum of Modern Art.

This exhibition honors a figure who has achieved a position of international renown within his field, while choosing to use San Francisco as base for his operations. And, as is so often the case, it honors a figure who remains controversial in his hometown, even as his international reputation continues to prosper. For this reason alone, it is of particular importance that the exhibition should open here in San Francisco.

Not only does the exhibition deal with specific projects of varied scope, but by bringing these projects together, it gives one a more comprehensive insight into the Halprin contribution — which is significant. He is not just a skilled follower in the grand tradition of northern California landscape enthusiasts, such as naturalist John Muir and landscape designer Thomas Church. While learning from them, Halprin has evolved rich schemes that endow our increasingly mechanized urban environments with human activity centers for participation, contemplation or repose. It is his capacity to first accept the urban landscape for what it is and then to go on to successfully humanize it that truly marks his significance.

It is with pleasure that the Museum presents this exhibition, and I thank Larry Halprin for the time and full support necessary to bring his work to a wider audience. Helene Fried proceeded with her usual skill and enthusiasm to complete this project — an extensive exhibition and catalog encompassing a lifetime of work.

As the Museum enters its second half-century, I am proud of the programs that have served the public so well. I am equally proud of the Museum's new Department of Architecture and Design. It is fitting that this first major exhibition of one designer's work is that of Lawrence Halprin — a man of the West, a man whose lifetime work pushed away the barriers of traditional design disciplines and created a totally new role, that of urban ecologist.

Henry T. Hopkins
Director
July 1986

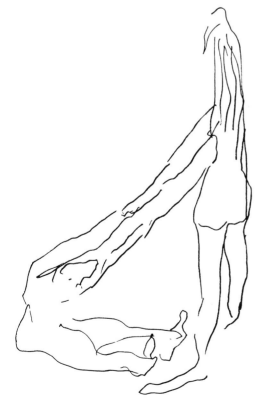

Introduction *by Helene Fried*

He is a man of great strength — emotional as well as physical. An overwhelming sense of curiosity and a compelling drive to affect change motivates his daily actions. Lack of barriers between his personal experience and his professional commitments characterize his life. Sometimes stern and gruff, he is also often gentle and quiet. Possessing a great imagination, he can initiate and respond to new ideas while also being capable of a deeply rooted stubbornness. Blessed with a compelling sense of his opportunity to play an important role, his actions have been guided by an appreciation of political and social issues, as well as the esthetic concerns of his profession.

Lawrence Halprin, more than anything, is a man of his times. He relishes the quest for better places where people can live and work and play. His ideas have evolved over a lifetime of study and travel, a lifetime rigorously pushing traditional boundaries while simultaneously maintaining traditional values.

While attending the University of Wisconsin in 1940 as a student in horticulture, Halprin came upon a book in the library that dramatically changed his life. Reading Christopher Tunnard's, *Gardens in the Modern Landscape*, he was struck by the significance of design in the environment. Imagine a twenty-three-year-old Halprin reading the following passage: "In a sick and suffering world...we have come to realize that the earthly paradise is unobtainable without the planner of garden and landscape. Society cannot afford to overlook his power to contribute to the life of the community. In his own medium he dispenses the two chief anodynes of life — art and play — without which we perish as surely as if we lack bread. That medium, the landscape, has taken on a new meaning which he alone, with his own special art and knowledge, can make especially clear to us. Let us give him the opportunity for creation.

"And here must end this exposition of a new approach to garden and landscape planning, two aspects of one major art of the twentieth century. The eighteenth century brought the landscape into garden planning; the twentieth century must bring the garden into the landscape. Through such a progress can arise the humanized landscape, the social conception of the countryside, and the garden of tomorrow."[1]

Halprin heeded the advice — he has brought the garden into the twentieth-century landscape. For the last fifty years, he has followed his own curiosity, combining professional skills, pushing aside tradition-bound answers, always learning, always growing. For this, we are grateful.

1. Christopher Tunnard, *Gardens in the Modern Landscape*, Architectural Press, London, 1938, 166.

A project of this scale and ambition requires the participation of many people whom I wish to acknowledge. It is the first major investigation of Halprin's lifetime work and both the catalog and exhibition demanded the commitment and stamina of many people.

Throughout more than a year of planning, Lawrence Halprin has been both generous and cooperative. My constant need to gather more and more information and materials — along with the many hours spent with him and members of his staff searching through the archives — was always met with enormous personal and professional generosity. Dee Mullen and Jeri Sulley of his office were particularly helpful. Most of all, without the able and willing assistance of Mendy Lowe, this project could not have come to fruition.

To those who contributed essays to this catalog — Jim Burns, Robert Maguire, Douglas Davis, Mayor Teddy Kollek, Dr. Joseph Henderson, Charles Moore, and Phyllis Tuchman — I am most grateful and appreciative, not only for their presentations, but also for their frankness about discussing their often personal reflections of their work with Halprin. Lynne Creighton Neall provided guidance and a thorough attitude as editor,

PERCEPTIONS OF NATURE.
Empathizing with the biological and emotional quality of a place allows Halprin to build a subconscious resource for future design. This "graphic memoir" depicts Phoenix Lake, a place near Halprin's home where he often hikes.

WATER. A major theme of Halprin's work is water, and one that he has used in a majority of his projects. This drawing is part of an ongoing study on water and its movement in response to other elements. Halprin has also investigated the environment of the water, in as much as it is defined by its boundaries. The drawings of water are both reactive and analytical — some responding to Halprin's appreciation of the place, others analyzing the movement and sounds of the water.

while Suzanne Anderson-Carey provided a design both compelling and insightful.

Frank O. Gehry and Greg Walsh designed an exciting exhibition installation, and the Museum wishes to thank Robert Graham, George Segal, and others for loans to the exhibition.

Lawrence Halprin: Changing Places is a project of great ambition and complexity. The museum staff demonstrated great skill and extraordinary commitment to the successful execution of both the catalog and exhibition. The Curatorial Department, led by Chief Curator Graham Beal, provided endless support and good will. Anne Munroe, Administrator, Curatorial Programs, supervised the scheduling, budget, and publication with the professional skill and cooperation that characterizes her work. Donna Graves, Curatorial Assistant, Lydia Tanji, and Debby Lawn worked with great enthusiasm on the seemingly endless details and arrange-

East...

cotton wood grove

corn field

start...

up the cliff

The footrace at sunrise from Shongopovi - 2nd mesa Sat. Aug 21 · 82 ....

NETWORKING. In nature, connections exist between the nest, the source of food, of water, and a place to sun; all serving biological, emotional, and functional needs. Aware of this in nature, Halprin designs links between places of working, living, shopping, and playing.

Stockholm ... Dancer's workshop ..... rehearsal @ stadsteatern ~ parades & changes

MOVEMENT AND CHOREOGRAPHY. All of Halprin's work emphasizes choreography, the design of movement through space, as a basic generating force in his planning of spaces and environments.

ments. Tina Garfinkel, Associate Registrar/ Exhibitions, arranged for the many drawings and models in the exhibition, while Kent Roberts, Gallery Superintendent, and his staff executed the ambitious exhibition design.

Robert Whyte, Director of Education, developed a multifaceted educational program; Kathleen Rydar, Director of Development, sought financial support with enthusiasm; Marcia Tanner, Director of Public Relations, and her staff worked effectively to bring the often complex ideas of Halprin to a wider audience; and Toby Kahn, Bookshop Manager, assisted in the development of the catalog.

I am most grateful to Henry T. Hopkins. His courage and vision established the Department of Architecture and Design, eventually leading to this and hopefully other ambitious and creative projects. To museum trustees, Thomas B. Swift and Frances Bowes, I am deeply appreciative of their ongoing support of the new department.

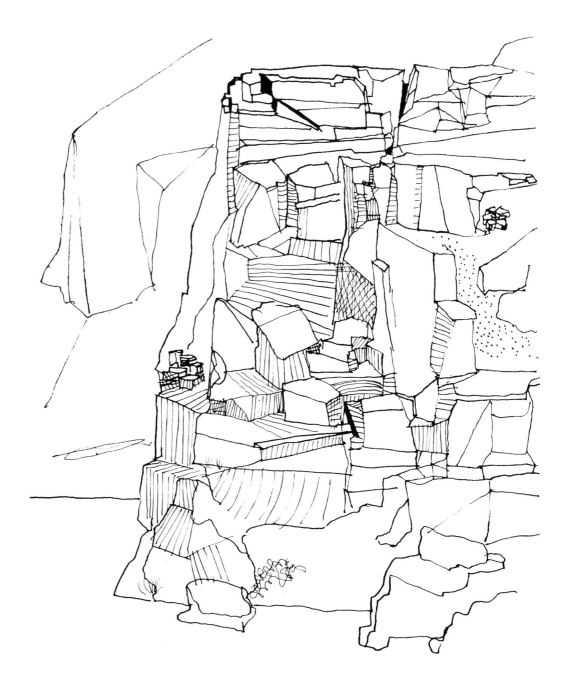

ECOLOGY OF FORM. Halprin is constantly studying the processes of nature — water, wind, and erosion — and their effects on the creation of forms and their placement in the natural landscape.

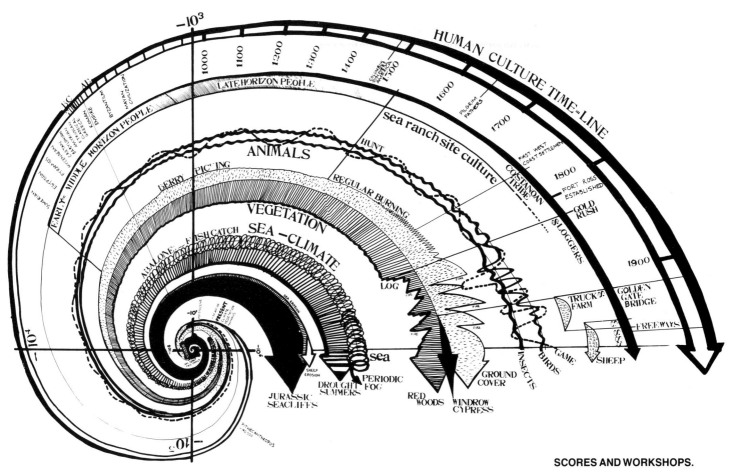

SCORES AND WORKSHOPS.
Halprin's use of scores, similar
to those used in music, is twofold:
as a way to motivate action from
one person to another and to
activate a process; or as a
way to record or summarize a
workshop or event. It is a method
of marking a broad range of human
activities. Workshops, often
generated by scores, are an
opportunity to bring people
together to solve problems or
create collective works of art.
Shown here is an "ecoscore"
for The Sea Ranch, prepared by
Tom Curtis, 1962.

Still Pools and Crashing Waves *by Charles Moore*

CHARLES MOORE *came to prominence when his work at The Sea Ranch, with Lawrence Halprin and Moore's firm of MLTW, attracted national attention and profoundly influenced the course of contemporary architecture. Since then, his architectural theories have found form in such buildings as the University of California, Santa Barbara, Faculty Club, 1968; Piazza d'Italia, New Orleans, 1978; the Hood Art Museum, Dartmouth College, Hanover, New Hampshire, 1985. Moore's publications include* The Place of Houses *(1974),* Dimensions: space, shape & scale in architecture *(1976), and* Body Memory and Architecture *(1977). He has taught at the University of California, Berkeley and Los Angeles, and Yale University, New Haven, Connecticut. He is currently teaching at the University of Texas, Austin.*

Workshop # 2: "Communities," 1968, The Sea Ranch, California. Students are led on environmental-awareness walks in which they walk blindfolded, experiencing their surroundings by senses other than sight.

**Far right:
The Sea Ranch, 1962, California. Rooflines of a cluster of condominiums directly relate to the natural forms of nearby cliffs.**

When I worked in Larry Halprin's office in the early 1960s, I wanted very much to become a landscape architect. Since then I've spent a great deal of time pondering the special attributes of landscape architecture: for one thing, there seems to be far more design drawings and far fewer technical ones than in most architectural offices, so more exciting stuff seems to be going on at once (at least in a place like Halprin's). But maybe more importantly, landscape architects are working, at least in part, with materials that grow, and decay, and change, not just in the inert stones and pipes of the architect's vocabulary. The frame of mind that goes with composing materials that don't stay put must be a very special one, rather like that of a teacher who introduces ideas, with no control over where the student will take them from there. For a special genius like Larry Halprin's, then, design becomes a matter not of controlled arrangement, but of exciting encounter. Life, you might say, is like a workshop, which is perhaps why the invention of the Taking Part process seemed to come so easily to Larry and to Jim Burns. Just as a workshop has its own dynamics, which you have to face without fear (or the workshop won't work), even so the design process in Larry Halprin's midst, requires confident movement through sometimes unexplored territory, and it doesn't do to panic when you can't get your bearings.

This essay about Larry Halprin is going to turn out to be in large part about myself, and I don't apologize for that. Interesting and important as Halprin's work is, what is for me the real importance is the power of the ideas, the unstoppable dynamics of his vision — a vision of humans experiencing with all our senses a richly dynamic natural world. One of the Halprin exercises I remember the most vividly from the early workshops was one where we moved around The Sea Ranch, on California's northern coast, deprived in turn of each one of our senses. We were first blindfolded, then our ears were plugged, then we were denied touch, and the temporary removal of each of our senses made the remaining ones, finally all of them, more important than ever.

In the plaza there should be events..... sculpture
shows - concerts - dance events with dancers all
over AND arriving to center space from above
down stairs around fountain ---

I first encountered Larry in 1963, when I entered a pair of little houses in a *Sunset* magazine competition. One of them was well enough received, but the other—a tiny cabin with a huge industrial window, a tar-paper roof, and a casually detachable smokestack— seems to have drawn heavy fire. Larry, who was on the jury, defended it, and the house received a special award. He later contacted me with the recommendation that our office, Moore, Lyndon, Turnbull, Whitaker (MLTW), do a project at The Sea Ranch, which he had begun to plan. MLTW was then in its very early stage, with not quite enough work yet to keep it busy; Larry's office, on the other hand, was humming with large and fascinating jobs. What thrilled me most was not only the extraordinary range of interesting commissions, but the chance that seemed to lie in each one to make some kind of real breakthrough.

By the late 1960s, I had become involved in an urban renewal of Larry's in downtown Portland, Oregon. Out of two parks that were to be created, Larry decided that one would be landscape and water, the other soft and green. Larry knew that I had done my Ph.D. dissertation on "Water in Architecture," and asked me to take on the landscape plot henceforth called Lovejoy Plaza. I was, of course, thrilled at the first chance I had to design a fountain since my dissertation. Larry had the image, inspired by a waterfall he loved in the High Sierra, of water splashing over rocky ledges. This resonated with images I carried of a cascade on slanted ledges just above Fallen Leaf Lake, near Lake

Lovejoy Plaza, 1965, Portland, Oregon. This erosion form reflects the quality and character of the High Sierra.

High Sierra Tarn, Yosemite National Park, California. Halprin often hiked the John Muir Trail where he developed many of his theories about the evolution of form.

Lovejoy Plaza, 1965, Portland, Oregon.

Tahoe, California. I take it as corroboration of the effectiveness of Larry's skills in inviting participation, that to this day when each of us lectures about Lovejoy, he shows his source and I show mine. The outcome of successful workshops is like that, with each participant confident of his own centrality, confident enough to be generous about the contributions of others.

I no longer remember who thought up what on Lovejoy Plaza. It was my notion, probably, that water would well up at the top higher than where one was sitting in order to give a sense of imminent inundation and then cascade down to a lower level. It was probably the idea of Jim Coleman, the job captain, that the whole park, which had to be constructed of concrete for economy, be poured behind two-by-six-inch board risers, for further economy. I remember going to Larry with my first plan of the water steps; I was very proud of them at the time, but I recall them now as being pathetically drab. Larry was enthusiastic, though, and didn't discourage me a bit when he suggested that I do them over completely, making them far more rich and complex and supportive of bright figures in the splashing water.

To me it is still an extraordinary feat that somehow, someway Larry managed to persuade the clients in Portland to accept those shapes whose likes they'd never seen before. There was only one part of the design

that (probably fortunately) he didn't persuade them to accept: originally, after the water had cascaded to the lower level and had flowed between stepping stones that were meant to let participants walk out into the middle of things, it swept around the lower basin into a swirling whirlpool straight out of Edgar Allan Poe. It was feared by the clients that this exciting maelstrom might suck up every detached infant in Portland, and it subsequently became a pool of quiet water. Probably just as well.

Larry's hope for the Lovejoy, and mine, was that people would feel close to it in a spirit that a British magazine had called "mental leaning out over," and that part worked well beyond our fondest expectations. Larry reported that at the dedication, two hippies (they were numerous in Portland then) slid down the cascade. Later, according to reports, there were two hippie weddings in the upper basin and so many premarital incidents that the residents of nearby high rises instituted a drive to replace the water with geraniums, or something pricklier. Fortunately, they never succeeded.

So that our fledgling architectural office would get some credit associated with Portland, we were asked to design a long and thin shelter with an irregular roof on the upper edge of the square, "like mountains above the water in Chinese painting," an art historian once said. Others were less kind: "an

Lovejoy Plaza, 1965, Portland, Oregon.

Lovejoy Plaza, 1965, Portland, Oregon. Steps echo rocky ledges of the High Sierra, and the fountain invites the public's participation.

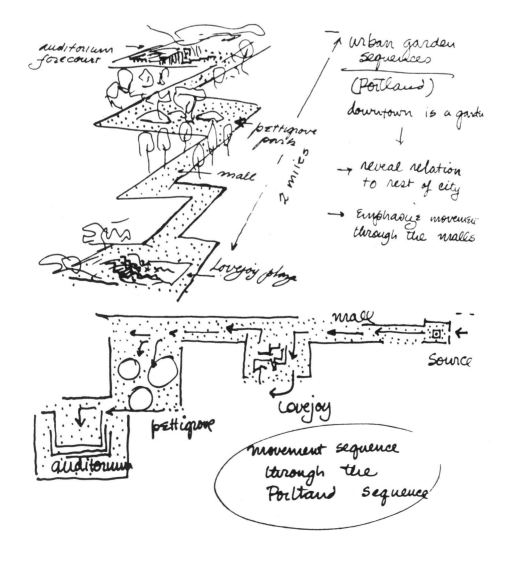

auditorium forecourt

pettigrove parks

2 miles

mall

Lovejoy plaza

urban garden sequences

(Portland)

downtown is a garden

↓

→ reveal relation to rest of city

→ Emphasize movement through the malls

mall

Source

Lovejoy

pettigrove

auditorium

movement sequence through the Portland sequence

Portland Open-Space Sequence, 1965, Portland, Oregon. The three open spaces offer a diversity of experiences for public use. Drawing by Lawrence Halprin.

overturned fruit basket run over by a truck," said one critic; "an architectural tantrum. Who threw that?" asked one of my Yale colleagues. But the fountain caught on and paved the way, I like to think, for the more dramatic successes of Larry's Auditorium Forecourt fountain in Portland and his Freeway Park in Seattle. For both of these Angela Danadjieva took on the role I played on the Lovejoy. Some future architectural historian will have fun analyzing the differences in these works as the cast of participants changed, as well as the continuities that attended Larry's own powerful presence. I guess I'm not really sure that the future historian will have any fun at all, since the expectations of a solo performance from the historian are at some odds with the realization that the design process is seldom, if ever, a solo flight. I enjoy the parallel with the Chinese painter who puts ink onto rice paper: there too the process is unpredictable; the brush loaded with ink touches the paper, and the ink flows out. The painter leaves the brush, or pulls it back, or moves it, in instant response to his medium, to get the effect he wants. As so the designer, working with the surprises of splashing water, as well as the visions of his clients and colleagues and the errant growth patterns of his plants, is engaged not nearly so much in God-like Creation (of the On-The-Seventh-Day-He-Rested sort) as in creative encounter, responding to the energies and the opportunities and even the mysteries of the moment.

While all the excitment was going on in Portland, work, which by now seems to have

Auditorium Forecourt (now Ira Keller Fountain), 1965, Portland, Oregon. The design of the fountain's upper level is drawn from glacial scouring typical of the High Sierra peaks. At the fountain's base are large concrete platforms that often serve as stages for public events.

Far left:
Seattle Freeway Park, 1970, Seattle. An urban park built over a freeway. Here, water rushing through a "gorge" drops almost fifty feet and masks traffic noise from below.

The Sea Ranch, 1962, Sonoma County, California. Drawing by Lawrence Halprin from his notebooks.

Sea Ranch –
Looking South – March 12th

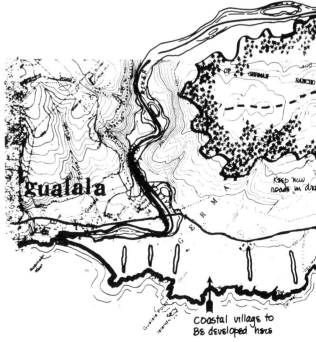

gualala

KEEP NEW
roads in dra

Coastal village to
BE developed here

been of an even more revolutionary sort, was going on at The Sea Ranch. There was an explosive excitement to the extraordinary combination of energies of Larry and his office: Al Boeke, the client's vice president, Fred Simpich, the more distant but supportive president, Marion Conrad presenting and representing it all, Reverdy Johnson writing the rules, and the architects, MLTW and Joseph Esherick's office, with Matthew Sylvia constructing the first buildings. Here again, I think it was Larry's landscape architect's sense of encounter with a hauntingly beautiful landscape that set the tone for all our efforts: we found ourselves saying that about our own condominium, which was meant neither to dominate the landscape, nor to be so dominated by it as to efface itself, but rather to come into a partnership with the landscape, to make something new that would be at home with what was there.

Below:
The Sea Ranch, 1962, Sonoma County, California. Summary score of basic ideas and philosophies for the development of The Sea Ranch.

Above:
The Sea Ranch, 1962, Sonoma County, California. In foreground is one of only a few pre-existing structures—a barn that has become a local "historical monument"; in background is the first Sea Ranch condominium cluster designed by Moore, Lyndon, Turnbull & Whitaker.

gualala river

all utilities to be underground

road along ridge line

in forest natural drainageways to be preserved & used as green fingers to the sea

keep houses back of trees

acquire this property for swimming

develop 3000' runway airport

corporation yard in this area

keep new roads in draws

No houses this far

STATE   HIGHWAY   101   GREAT MENO

Meadows kept open

forest

keep coast open
for riding, hiking, access to water and for visual easement.

Condominium here

cluster all houses on ocean terrace
in linear clusters, condominiums and squares.

major Public Beach - develop stair access

area for lodge & inn

keep flat area open as visual easement

north

Preserve Black Point as permanent open space

SEA RANCH

Lawrence Halprin & Associates

pacific ocean

·5000 ACRES·

☞ LOCATIONAL SCORE

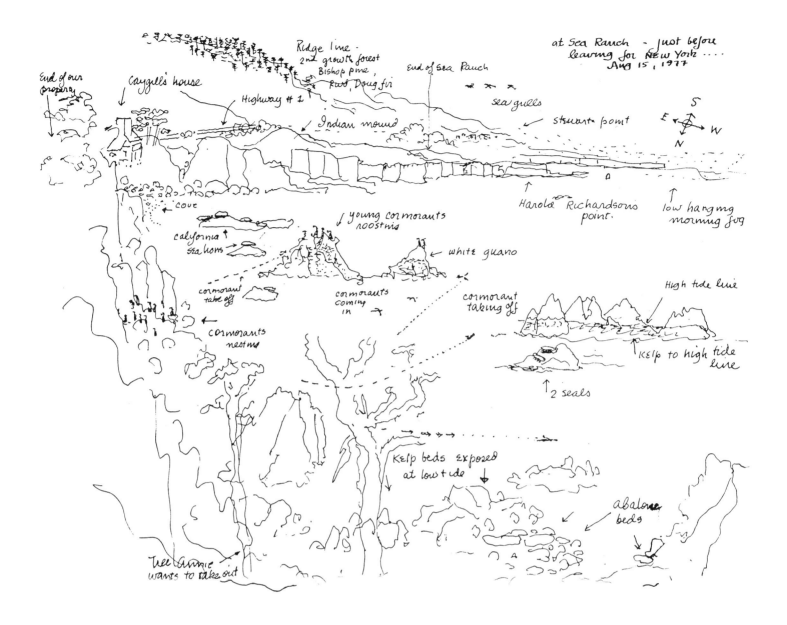

The Sea Ranch, 1962, Sonoma County, California. Drawing by Lawrence Halprin.

Larry's planning effort started with a marvelously complete survey of what was there—the sun and the wind and the fog and the land and the vegetation, the latter two already products of human intervention over the last hundred years. Richard Reynolds, a geologist in Larry's office, rose to the demanding occasion with a superbly complete recording of the existing conditions; but what was most impressive to me was the way that the inevitable intervention in the magnificent (but already intervened-in) landscape was seen as an action over time, a continuing partnership that would need to be modified as the years went by, actions and reactions that would develop in an ongoing composition, the way a good gardener develops a garden across the years. Somewhere along the way, things went a little awry at The Sea Ranch, and Larry's role mostly ended, to be replaced by a long, long duel between The Sea Ranch homeowners and the California state bureaucracy. The duel came to a dazzling climax when some 1,300 trees were cited (I think it was a misdemeanor, not really a felony), and doomed to decapitation or death for their temerity in growing up between Highway 1 and the sea, compromising what meanwhile had been deemed the inevitable and eternal right of every motorist along Highway 1 to have a continuous and unobstructed view of the water.

It would be hard to find an attitude more at odds with the sense of planning that Larry represents. More recent chapters in this continuing saga are less harrowing. Twenty years after its beginnings, there seems to have been a general realization at The Sea Ranch: first, that the original ideas of Larry and the others were important and correct; and second, implied in the first, that things change and that new visions are required for the next twenty years. Land has become far more expensive, building lots have become smaller, houses are closer together and influenced by one another, as well as by the great sweeps of landscape.

One of my favorite images of our time from The Sea Ranch is the tide pool. Strange and wonderful little creatures flourish in the still,

NOTES & COMMENTS about
DESIGN @ the SEA RANCH   — FEB 85
Larry Halprin

My concerns about the Sea Ranch as it
is now as compared with how it used to be is
largely based on the shift from a sense of
wildness & a relation to nature to a kind of
suburban image — no longer wild & NOT even a
unique built environment any more. that is:
the changes that have occurred are a compromise
not a positive and strong image of man made
with nature to the enhancement of each.
    I think we need a shift from overall
plan & overall image to precinct — the in-
between doesn't work. anymore. & the single house doesn't
                                                  either.
    At the beginning a series of overall
criteria were established :

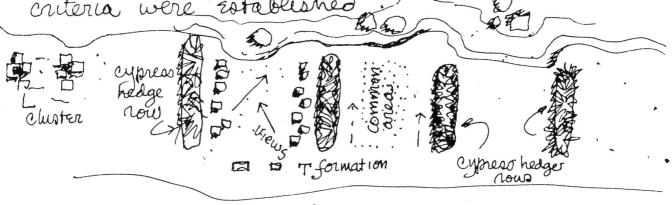

Hway 1

THE **T** formation was ①
    it kept: the houses parallel to the hedge rows
of cypress , the meadows as large common areas
the ocean front open to preserve the views.
② The idea of clustering was established
    There were several kinds of clusters:
    Ⓐ condominiums in farm house type
                        groupings

Far right:
Workshop #5: "LA Spectacular,"
1981, The Sea Ranch, California.
Aerial view of Driftwood City.

tidal pools at the edge of the ocean. As the waves wash in, the quiet pools are obliterated in a wonderful froth of raging waters, which, in their turn subside as the pool grows still, and the remarkable creatures wiggle around again. I find myself identifying with the still pool, peopled by weird and amazing creatures. Most famous architects of our time I identify with the crashing waves. Larry seems equally at home with the still pool or the crashing waves, which is as it should be. If I am right about Larry's design strength as a continuing encounter, the to and fro has a lot to do with the Chinese principles of yin and yang, of the mutually necessary acts of pressing and receiving, or creating and absorbing, but above all staying alive for the reciprocating ebb and flow of events in the built forms that follow.

Though the designs for Portland and The Sea Ranch were made over twenty years ago, some of my happiest moments since have been spent with Larry at The Sea Ranch where he has an unfindable house that Bill Turnbull and I helped with, and a wonderful studio that is very carefully undazzling, so that making something new is not altogether overpowered by the magnificence of the surrounding scenery. Some of those times have been at workshops, others working on competitions for three plazas, and schemes for a garden and

hotel and office project. So far not a one of them has been built, but hope is not dead.

The first workshop was run in the late sixties by Larry and his wife Anna for dancers and architects. Our role was to help show people around The Sea Ranch, a simple enough task but one that produced lasting effects on me. Coming from the static academic atmosphere of an architecture school, where people dealt inevitably in classroom abstractions to a workshop, where architecture and the environment were things you moved in and out of and touched and saw and walked blindfolded through and heard and felt, and most of all the dancers and a few of the architects took off their clothes so as to approach the surroundings more closely...all this was a heavy shift, and seemed, and still seems to me, to be getting things closer to what's right. What got built over a couple of days at the end of that workshop was a set of individual constructions on the beach, which added up to a village, much fuller of symbolic implication than "real" architects were building at the time, much more expressive of the dreams of the temporary inhabitants. My most vivid recollection of that village is of a four-legged platform out in the chilly water, a briefly inhabited altar in the teeth of the sea, for four men to greet the sunset.

Workshop #2: "Communities,"
1968, The Sea Ranch, California.
Driftwood platform.

Pioneer Square Competition
Model, 1980, Portland, Oregon.
With Charles Moore.

Far right:
Bunker Hill Competition, 1980, Los
Angeles. Looking east from Grand
Avenue into the main courtyard of
proposed project. Drawing by
Lawrence Halprin.

Many years later, Larry ran another work-shop at The Sea Ranch for my class at the University of California, Los Angeles. In one, which up to that time had notably failed to coalesce, Larry performed miracles of developing common cause as the students built and then recorded a curious bipolar beach village, part chaos and part strong hierarchic order that seemed to reveal more about themselves to each other than anything else had to that point. Again, what people built and how and what they felt seemed to come together to bring increased clarity to each.

Other experiences in Larry's studio at The Sea Ranch had many of the aspects of a workshop, but were instead devoted to the production of competition designs. Admittedly, we never won any, but we made some interesting schemes. One was a design, in an invited competition, for Pioneer Square in Portland, Oregon. We made a plaza principally devoted to a fountain that was mostly Larry's design—stepped a little like Lovejoy, but with more elaborate waterways, a grotto, and considerable planting. The fountain was ringed by buildings—a restaurant, conservatory, colonnade, and a little stage in a tower which were mostly designed by me, though it was all worked out by both of us together.

Two small parks and a grand boulevard for a limited competition at Bunker Hill in

downtown Los Angeles gave us an even more splendid stage to try to make a place where people would feel comfortable gathering at the feet of skyscrapers. In the parks were places to sit and eat and look at theater and at passers-by, surrounded by all manner of water, from streams quietly running down wide stairs to bombastic baroque fountains, with an open space filled with cafés and monuments along a boulevard. The long open space, at first too closely connected with the boulevard to be very interesting, came alive when Larry started to see it as a stepped-up quayside, a shore against which a car in the boulevard might temporarily moor. That image was typical Halprin…an open-ended one that allowed for all sorts of possibilities, while it set very loose limits on what might appear. The one limit he was anxious to set was that what was built would not look just *like* something else…no classical temples, please, or Gothic furbelows, or Victorian doodads. He did allow me to squeeze an intaglio impression of a Victorian house of the sort that used to exist on Bunker Hill into the mirrored face of a 100-foot-high pavilion—one of the few instances I can recall where his desire to be agreeable overcame his desire to do it right. Or maybe he liked it.

One of my fondest memories is of a several-day mission to work on the landscape for a project in Pasadena, California for Rob Maguire, the client for the Bunker Hill project

Bunker Hill Competition, 1980, Los Angeles. Drawing by Lawrence Halprin.

Bunker Hill Competition, 1980, Los Angeles. Rendering by Carlos Diniz.

and a man we much admire and try hard to
please. The project included, at that stage
a great crescent of an arcade, three stories
high, drawn opposite the wonderful sixty-
year-old Beaux-Arts city hall of Pasadena—a
marvelously airy, baroque construction that
comes off Hispanic (for all its French detail)
and somehow lushly tropical. This time I was
to do the arcade, and Larry would act as critic.
He made the rules: arches would be okay,
provided they did not recall anything, not even
the city hall, especially not the city hall, not
Spanish, not baroque, not Romanesque, not
anything except semicircular. I did them over
and over, too eclectic, too flaccid, too dull,
until Larry finally said that one would be all
right. It was worth it, I think, and I believe we
really captured the essence of Pasadena,
though it's not, finally, going to happen that
way. I like to think that it's because it's too
wonderful to be built just yet.

There have been other joint projects too,
including a secret garden next to the

**Plaza Las Fuentes, 1982,
Pasadena, California. Model showing design of courtyards relating
to early California vernacular
architecture and landscape. In the
background is dome of the
Pasadena City Hall. With Moore,
Ruble & Yudell.**

37

Library Gardens, Los Angeles
Central Library, 1983, Los Angeles.
The gardens are part of a large
project including the library itself,
designed in 1926 by Bertram
Goodhue, and currently under-
going restoration by Hardy,
Holzman & Pfeiffer. Drawing by
Lawrence Halprin.

Library Gardens, Los Angeles Central Library, 1983, Los Angeles. Drawing of plan by Lawrence Halprin.

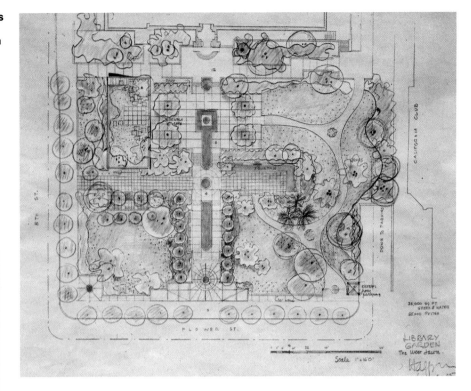

Los Angeles Central Library for Rob Maguire, and I hope there will be more. It's a veritable fountain of youth, this Halprin continuing creative encounter. It is certainly full of yin and yang, and the splendors of oriental balanced thought, but I don't want to leave the impression that Larry's connection to the world that grows and changes is that of an oriental mystic. The wisdom from both, I guess, contains more of the Talmud than the Tao. Larry would insist, I suspect, that the wisdom is Old Testament, or, more modernly, openness held aloft on chutzpah. For all the wonders of his many works, it is his visions and his deeds, his opening up of the world to many kinds of people that constitute most of the dimensions of his achievements.

The *How* of Creativity: Scores & Scoring *by Jim Burns*

JIM BURNS *designs and conducts Take Part processes nationally for communities, neighborhoods, schools, and user groups. An alumnus of Halprin's 1968 "Experiments in Environment" workshop, he was formerly senior editor of* Progressive Architecture *and an associate in Lawrence Halprin & Associates. Burns has written extensively on environmental design and planning, including a critical biography of The Sea Ranch, which is soon to be published by Van Nostrand Reinhold Publishing Co., Inc.*

Thirty-seven years ago, Lawrence Halprin wrote a brief piece for the San Francisco dance magazine, *Impulse,* about using garden designs to liberate people's kinetic sense. "As a framework for movement activities the garden can influence our lives tremendously," he wrote, noting that his gardens were "designed to determine the movement of people in them."[1] Halprin contrasted the classic garden with its carefully balanced vistas and artfully arranged focal points with contemporary, more free-form gardens that encourage vigorous participation in a wider range of activities. The classic garden was compared to the precision choreography of the traditional ballet, while the modern garden was praised for opening up a whole new scope of movement and kinetic possibilities.

Without realizing it at the time, Halprin had touched on a concept that would germinate for two decades before reaching maturity in a theory of creative process—the *how* of people's creativity, not the *what* of what they create. During the twenty-year gestation period, he was nevertheless working through the process in many of his professional activities. In creating plans and designs to change environments that people would use, he was employing processes and techniques that he would ultimately attempt to codify his theories. In this he was like Molière's M. Jourdain in "Le Bourgeois Gentilhomme," who delightedly discovered in his middle years that he had been speaking prose all his life. Halprin's "prose" consisted of the sketches, designs, plans, models, and construction documents that produced designed environments, as well as early graphic scenarios for dance and theater events.

Halprin had an advantage over most practitioners in coming to terms with the *how* of creativity. Because of his work with wife Anna Halprin and her avant-garde San Francisco Dancers' Workshop, he spent a lot of time collaborating with people in areas of art seldom encountered by most landscape architects: composers, musicians, scene and lighting designers, script writers, performers, choreographers. The discoveries he made in these experiences elaborated how he thought about designing places that can engage people's senses, so that their "lives

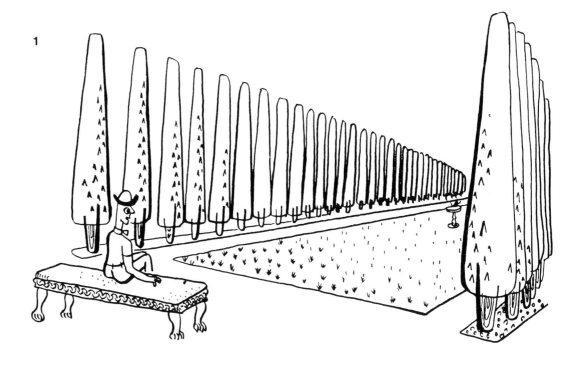

1

2

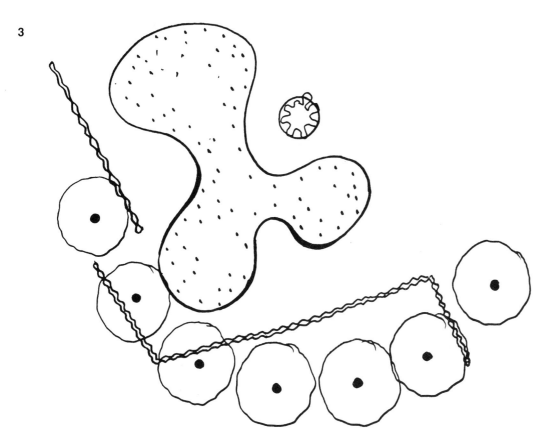

3

Lawrence Halprin's sketches for a 1949 article show that he was already thinking how landscape design could "score" people's activities in space. A classic garden (1) makes people passive viewers. It is compared to a traditionally choreographed ballet (2) in which the audience does not participate. A freely designed contemporary garden plan (3) "choreographs" people's participation in a variety of kinetic possibilities.

Far right:
Nicollet Avenue, Minneapolis.

can be given the continuous sense of dance."[2] This, in turn, led him to devise a graphic "motation" system of movement through space for use in assessing and designing people's environments. His motation system for the redesign of Nicollet Avenue in Minneapolis is shown here. The next time you stroll through San Francisco's Levi's Plaza, Portland, Oregon's Lovejoy Plaza, or Seattle's Freeway Park, you may experience what a powerful impact the idea of choreographing the designed environment for people's movement has had on Halprin's work.

Nicollet Avenue, Minneapolis.

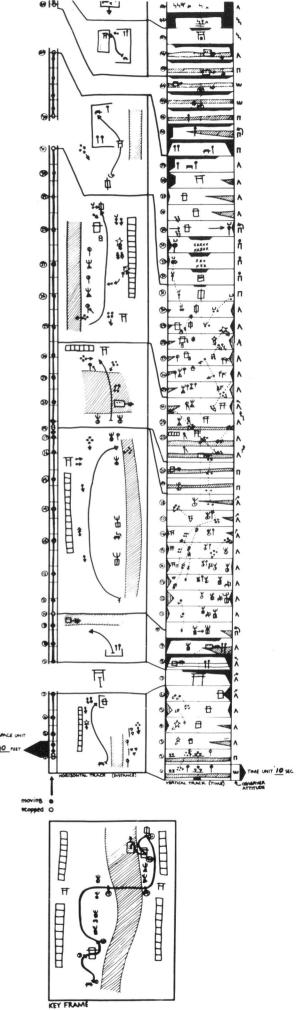

Halprin's "motation" score for the redesign of Nicollet Avenue in Minneapolis indicated graphically through a system of symbols the qualities of experience that were designed for that environment.

Experiments in Environment, Workshop #2: "Driftwood," 1968.

"Experiments in Environment" were month-long explorations conducted by the Halprins in 1966 and 1968 that helped participants make discoveries about themselves, and their environments.

The decade of the 1960s was one of self-searching and exploration of root impulses as much as it was of flower power and political upheaval. Some environmental design professionals, writers and practitioners alike, were examining primal influences, innovative design concepts, and projecting past their drafting boards to explore the *how* of creativity and how process affects results. This approach was different from the customary, linear, object-oriented attitudes of most designers and planners, who put all their attention on the products of their labors and none on the processes by which they were achieved. Anna and Larry Halprin were intensely absorbed in the *how* of creative processes, and, with friends and colleagues such as architect Charles Moore, they originated "Experiments in Environment," a multidisciplinary summer series of events that in 1966 plunged people deep into the experience of human/environment relationships. This proved such a potent and fruitful way of discovering and experiencing that a second "Experiments in Environment" was conducted in 1968 (with Gestalt therapist Paul Baum), exploring the even deeper waters of how family relationships develop and communities evolve.

Experiments in Environment, Workshop #2: "Graphix," 1968.

Experiments in Environment, Workshop #2: "Graphix," 1968.

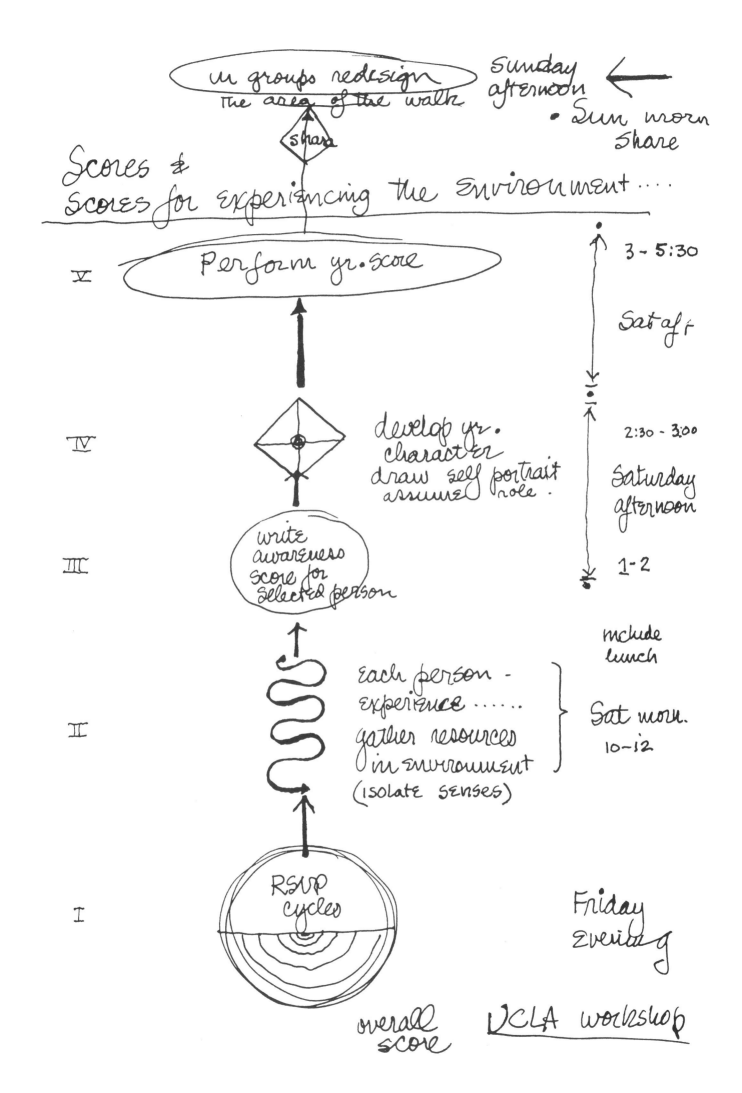

in groups redesign
the area of the walk

share

Sunday afternoon ←

• Sun morn
Share

Scores &
Scores for experiencing the environment....

V   Perform yr. score

3 - 5:30

Sat aft

IV   develop yr.
character
draw self portrait
assume role.

2:30 - 3:00

Saturday
afternoon

1 - 2

III   write awareness score for selected person

II   Each person -
experience ......
gather resources
in environment
(ISOLATE SENSES)

include
lunch

Sat morn.
10 - 12

I   RSVP cycles

Friday
evening

overall
score

UCLA workshop

46

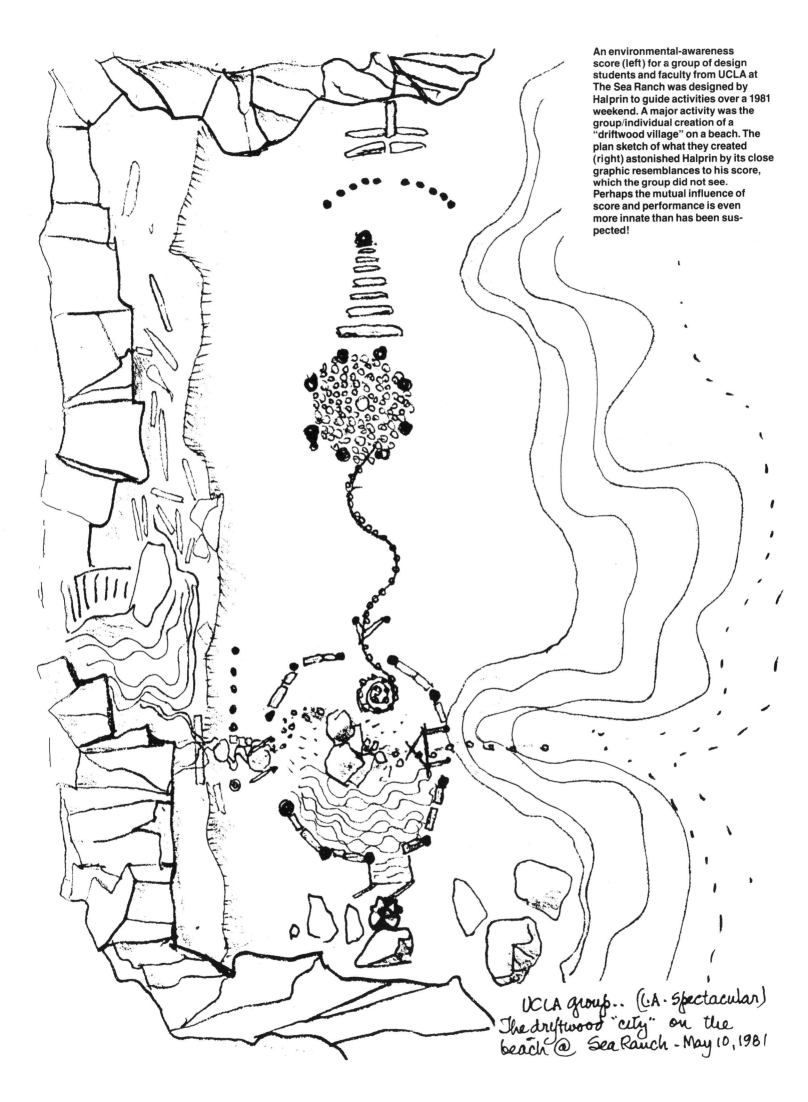

An environmental-awareness score (left) for a group of design students and faculty from UCLA at The Sea Ranch was designed by Halprin to guide activities over a 1981 weekend. A major activity was the group/individual creation of a "driftwood village" on a beach. The plan sketch of what they created (right) astonished Halprin by its close graphic resemblances to his score, which the group did not see. Perhaps the mutual influence of score and performance is even more innate than has been suspected!

UCLA group.. (L.A. Spectacular) The driftwood "city" on the beach @ Sea Ranch - May 10, 1981

This 1971 score for the kiddush ceremony in a California temple guided the congregation and other participants in a contemporary version of the ancient Jewish ritual for consecrating the Sabbath. The variant spelling "kadosh" provided symbols for the various performers. The spatial and time sequences were based on the symbol of the Star of David. The elements of space, participants, activity, and ritual formed a matrix for performance that people shared in both sacred and secular rites.

SCORE

for ANN HALPRIN
and the DANCER'S WORKSHOP

KADOSH   at TEMPLE SINAI

Friday, February 12, 1971

SCORE OBJECTIVE

a relation of sequential order of activities...
making visible the relationship between
    performers and congregation, in space

PEOPLE SYMBOLS

K   Cantor

A   assembled congregants

D   dancers

O   Officers of congregation

SH   Sam Harav

in Hebrew prayers (especially from medieval times) traditionally the first letter of each line added up to a symbolic meaning

MASTER SCORE

SPATIAL AND SEQUENTIAL ORDER

secular space   sacred space

SEQUENCE OF EVENTS

space	participants	activity
1 ⬡	K A D O S H	singing, dancing, folk dancing
2 ⬡	K D&A O SH D&SH&K	chants lead minyans of ten enter sacred space enters sacred space washing ritual; anointing
3 ⬡	SH D D	blessing light the lights readings from the Torah
4 ⬡	SH&D	Kaddish

space	participants	activity
5 ✡	D D&SH	relight lights personal affirmations, prayers
6 ✡	D&SH D&O&A SH	welcome bride; song, dance, instruments bride enters
7 ✡	D SH&A&O	chant: Kadosh Adonai Shema Shema
8 ✡	K A D O S H	myrtle procession to secular space for food sharing, chanting

In structuring the activities and formats that people would perform in "Experiments in Environment," Halprin discovered (as he had begun to in his earlier work with dance and theater) that he was more conscious about using the "prose" he had been employing in his professional and creative life. He paid closer attention to the processes that he and his colleagues were pursuing. This investigation evolved into theories about how art—in its larger definition—is made, how people can be creative together. These were finally articulated in his 1969 book *The RSVP Cycles.*

The RSVP theory of creativity is quadripartite but interdependent, so that each of its four elements influence and shape the others. They are *resources*, the aspects of individuals, community, environment, society, culture, economics that we have to understand and deal with in each given situation; *scores*, the activity-generating devices and formats that carry the process along; *performance*, the using of resources and scores to be creative and achieve results; and *valuaction*, a made-up word meaning continual evaluation of activities and accomplishments through all parts of the process, with an emphasis on action to alter, synthesize, and refine so that people are achieving what they need to achieve. This essay concentrates mostly on *scores*, since this is the element that activates people and can give the appropriate (or inappropriate) qualities to what they do.

Halprin's discovery, like M. Jourdain's, excited him and enlarged his comprehension of people's capabilities when engaged in appropriate processes. The idea of scores, in particular, seized his imagination, for scores can be the organizing matrix for many kinds of activities from day-to-day planning to events embodying fantasy and celebration. Scores are indications of people's actions in time and space. These three elements—activity, time, place—combine to provide a format for performance. In Halprin's profession, a site plan or building plan is the basic example for a score that, when performed, results in a new environment or structure. The new environment can be a three-dimensional score in the manner it influences the way people live, work, and play. This is the "prose" Halprin had been using for years, just as choreographic notations were Anna Halprin's "prose."

A more familiar illustration of the score is the music score, more specifically the operatic score-libretto, in which many of the possibilities of scores are embodied. The music score, as we know, is a graphic instruction from the composer to the players of which notes are to be played, in what kind of sequence, and how they are to be played (what tempi, nuances, emphasis, etc.). The music score is inevitably a kind of collective creativity, for if performers do not exist to execute and interpret it, it remains a mute scrap of paper.

In an intensive 1974 design-awareness workshop for federal bureaucrats conducted by Round-House for the National Endowment for the Arts, specially designed notebooks acted as participants' score for the workshop as well as their individual journals of their experiences. The front and back covers show the score for an important event, an awareness walk in Washington.

IL TROVATORE

ACT IV.

THE PUNISHMENT.

SCENE I—A wing of the palace of Aliaferia; in the angle, a tower with window secured by iron bars. Night; dark and clouded.

(Enter LEONORA and RUIZ, enveloped in cloaks.)

Ruiz   (in an undertone).

Here stay we;

Yonder's the tower where are confined the prisoners for state offences;

Hither they brought him whom we are seeking.

Leonora.

Go thou:

Leave me here; be not anxious for my safety;

Perchance I yet may save him.

        (RUIZ retires.)

Afraid for me? Secure

And ready are my defences!

(She gazes upon a jewel which she wears on her right hand.)

In this dark hour of midnight

I hover round thee near approaching.

Unknown to thee, love! Ye moaning breezes around me playing.

In pity aid me, my sighs to him conveying!

ATTO IV.

IL SUPPLIZIO.

SCENA I—Un' ala del palazzo dell' Aliaferia—all' angolo una torre, con finestre assicurate da spranghe di ferro. Notte oscurissima.

(Si avanzano due personne ammentellate; sono RUIZ LEONORA.)

Ruiz   (sommessamente).

Siam giunti:

Ecco la torre, ove di stato

Gemono i prigionieri.—Ah! l'infelice

Ivi fu tratto!

Leonora.

Vanne.

Lasciami, nè timor di me te prenda—

Salvarlo io potrò, forse.

        (RUIZ si allontana.)

Timor di me?—Sicura,

Presta è la mia difesa!

(I suoi occhi figgonsi ad una gemma che le fregia la man destra.)

In questa oscura

Notte ravvolta, presso a te son io,

E tu nol sai! Gemente

Aura, che intorno spiri,

Deh, pietosa gli arreca i miei sospiri.

D'AMOR SULL' ALI ROSEE — *ON ROSY WINGS OF LOVE*   Air. (Leonora)

D'a-mor sull'a - li ro-se - e   Van-ne, so-spir do-len - te,
On ro-sy wings of love de - part, Bear-ing my heart's sad wail - ing,

Del pri-gio-nie-ro mi - se-ro Con - for-ta l'e - gra-men-te.— Com'
Vis - it the pris'ner's lone - ly cell, Con - sole his spir-it fail-ing.— Let

au - ra di spe - ran - za   A - leg-gia in quel - la stan - za. Lo
hope's soft whis-pers— wreath - ing   A - round him, com - fort breath - ing, Re-

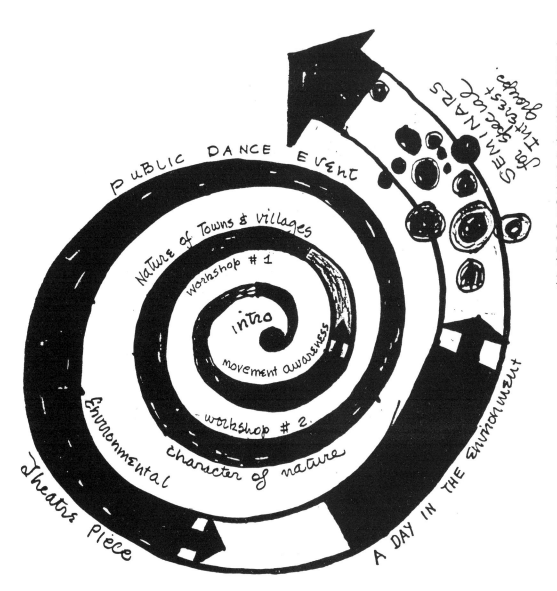

PUBLIC DANCE EVENT

SEMINARS for special groups

Nature of Towns & Villages

Workshop # 1

intro

movement awareness

workshop # 2.

Environmental character of nature

Theatre Piece

A DAY IN THE ENVIRONMENT

The spiraling nature of this 1981 score for "A Search for Living Myths," a collective process conducted by Anna and Lawrence Halprin, displays an archetypal graphic form symbolizing evolution from germination through physical and spiritual development toward a future of discovery. This score was for the first phase in the development of a ritual to exorcise Mount Tamalpais, which had been the locale of a series of brutal murders. The ritual became "Circle the Mountain," which was then recycled through several scores to become "Circle the Earth," a performance dedicated to world peace taken to many communities by Anna Halprin and the Tamalpa Institute.

The page from Cammarano's libretto for Verdi's *Il Trovatore* reproduced here exhibits a number of potentials for scores. The libretto itself is a score—the indication of action and qualities of the drama, its playscript. The music score is the over-riding lyric aspect of the drama that provides the arias, ensembles, set pieces, recitatives, choruses, overtures, and intermezzi that invigorate the libretto with the magic dimension of music. Within these two major scores are sub-scores: scores for the scenic or architectural setting ("A wing of the palace of Aliaferia"); time and environment scores ("Night; dark and clouded"); costume scores ("Enter Leonora and Ruiz, enveloped in cloaks"); acting scores ("Ruiz, in an undertone"); activity scores ("Ruiz retires"; "She gazes upon a jewel, which she wears on her right hand"). The music score gives the notes and orchestration that the singers and players must produce, and also the qualities of performance desired by Verdi. Within the structure of these scores, the conductor, singers, orchestra, chorus, stage director, and scene and costume designers express their own talents and creativity to the best of their abilities. That's what makes it interesting; one

performance of this beloved "chestnut" being quite different from another. Even a modest sub-score such as "Ruiz retires" can be performed in many ways. In a traditional production, Ruiz might walk off stage, slink off backward, or rush off at a fevered pace. A more innovative (or self-indulgent) director might have him crawl off on hands and knees, or jump into the palace moat and swim off. In a production transposed to modern times, Ruiz might roar off on his Harley-Davidson.

This illustrates a characteristic of scores to which Halprin has devoted considerable thought—their openness or closedness. An open score is one in which the scorer provides a minimum of instruction or clues and leaves the execution of the scores mainly to the performer. The stage is set, as it were, but the performance develops and emerges as it is performed. Keeping to our musical analogy, scores by John Cage tend to be open and aleatory. Contrasted is the closed score, in which the scorer makes practically all the determinations, and the performer is required to follow. Halprin suggests a scale of openness and closedness for scores, ranging from "0" (most open) to "10" (most closed).

Far left:
The music score and libretto for "Il Trovatore" by Verdi and Cammarano exhibit many qualities and potentials of scoring for people's performances.

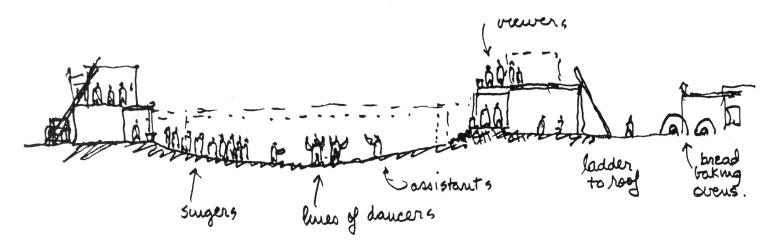

viewers

singers

lines of dancers

assistants

ladder
to roof

bread
baking
ovens.

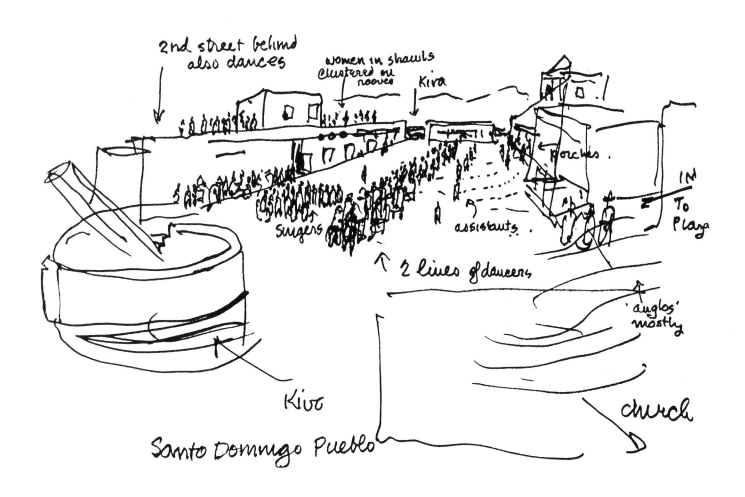

2nd street behind
also dances

women in shawls
clustered on
rooves

Kiva

porches.

IN
TO
Plaza

singers

assistants.

2 lines of dancers

'anglos'
mostly

Kiva

Santo Domingo Pueblo

church

Accomplished score designers will be able to locate their score precisely on this scale, so that its open/closed qualities will be appropriate to the situation and to the people performing the scores. Appropriateness is the watchword here. There is no inherent superiority of an open score over a closed score; the test is how it helps people to respond best to the situation. Designing a score to help people plan a medical center, for instance, would require a relatively closed score; there would be too many technological and potentially life-threatening considerations for scores toward the "0" end of the scale to be appropriate. Conversely, if a score is designed to liberate people's feelings of fantasy or festivity, an open score might be just the thing to involve them in the process of staging and performing the celebration together.

The more open a score is the more it activates processes that are exploratory, experimental, or designed to increase people's awareness and sensitivities in various situations. Scores that are open to the broadening of people's perceptions of process and creativity have been used in as disparate workshops as one for the National Endowment for the Arts to increase the awareness of the design process among federal bureaucrats, and a multidisciplinary workshop in Hakone, Japan, in which artists, writers, performers, and academics spent a week together exploring atavistic roots of community and creativity. Many of the sub-scores in these open-scored processes have to do with the liberation of fantasy and the exploration of deep personal and group emotions. As such, they tend frequently to reflect evocative themes and rituals that have characterized people's communal activities over the centuries and whose counterparts can be discerned in the religious rites and folkways of many cultures. Halprin says of these more open-scored processes that if they have a general objective, it "would be to release archetypal images from deep inside participants—both individually and as a group. Its intent therefore is to discover basic things about the world and ourselves and reveal them to each other. The sharing, for me, is significant and is a form of art."[3]

Kiva at the
East end of the
plaza —
one clan around &
in the Kiva after
they finished the
CORN Dance
        Monday Dec 28-80

Halprin's sketches of the performance of the Corn Dance at the Santo Domingo pueblo near Santa Fe are a record of a ritualistic activity whose score is buried in the mists of time and tradition, but kept alive by the religious leaders of the community.

Three serpent scores show how open and closed scores can influence performances differently in a similar situation. (1) An extremely closed score as warning. (2) A slightly more open score giving more information, including time. (3) An even more open score, giving reasons for the score and characteristics of a potential performer (the rattlesnake), thus giving the recipient more confidence.

1

2

3

The three little serpent scores illustrated here show how open and closed scores can influence people differently in a similar situation. The first is totally closed and unambiguous; it is a direct warning and rates a "10" on Halprin's scale. The second is a little more open, about "8.5"; it is more specific about the serpent you are to avoid (presumably you can congregate with other reptiles, if you wish), and adds a time frame for your activities. The third serpent score takes you into the scorer's confidence and gives a lot of information on why you are being asked to avoid rattlesnakes, and gives resource data on them; armed with this information, you can perform the score with more security and aplomb. This would rate about "7" on the scale. The effect of each of these scores on potential performers would be different: alarmed for the first; concerned for the second; confident for the third. So we see that the nature and quality of the score—open or closed—will have a direct influence on the quality and appropriateness of the performance.

Lest it be thought that scores are always communicated graphically and verbally, I should point out that many varieties of media and actions can be utilized. "Legend says that when Buddha was about to die he asked that his ashes be buried on a stupa; to explain what that was, he folded his tunic in a square, placed his inverted begging bowl on top, and finished off with his walking stick."[4] Thus, Buddha gave a score vocally and by demonstration. A three-

TRINITY RIVER STUDY

ACTIVITY SCORE

The activity score for the Trinity River as it passes through Fort Worth was based on recommendations from a community planning workshop with residents, community leaders, and merchants in that city (1969). Many of these elements were realized and are now in use.

LEGEND

KEY TO SYMBOLS.

☐ ACTIVITY POINT

▨ COMMUNITY RELATED ACT.

◫ ROAD BRIDGE CROSSING TRINITY RIVER

⊕ PARKING

◐ MIN. RAILROAD TERMINAL OR STATION

⬤ SUBWAY TO CITY CENTER

● RESIDENTIAL

△ INDUSTRIAL

⚠ INDUSTRIAL/COMMERCIAL

◬ COMMERCIAL

--- TRAIL SYSTEM

---·--- MIN. RAILROAD

▰▰▰ TRINITY PARK

(A) PEDESTRIAN   (C) BICYCLE
(B) EQUESTRIAN   (D) PARKWAYS AS NEC.

KEY TO ACTIVITIES.

1	FOREST PARK ZOO	13	URBAN LAKE 2
2	OPEN MKT. & DAM	14	**ACTIVITY & INFO. CTR.** ENT. TO PARK SYSTEM
3	BOAT HIRE DOCK		
4	WINDMILL THEATER		
5	DUCK POND		
6	EQUESTRIAN AREA		
7	URBAN LAKE 1 AT JUNCT. OF EAST & WEST FORKS OF TRINITY		
8	BELVEDERE		
9	TESCO		
10	OVERLOOK		
11	GO-CART & SPEEDWAY TRACK		
12	COMMUNITY CENTER		

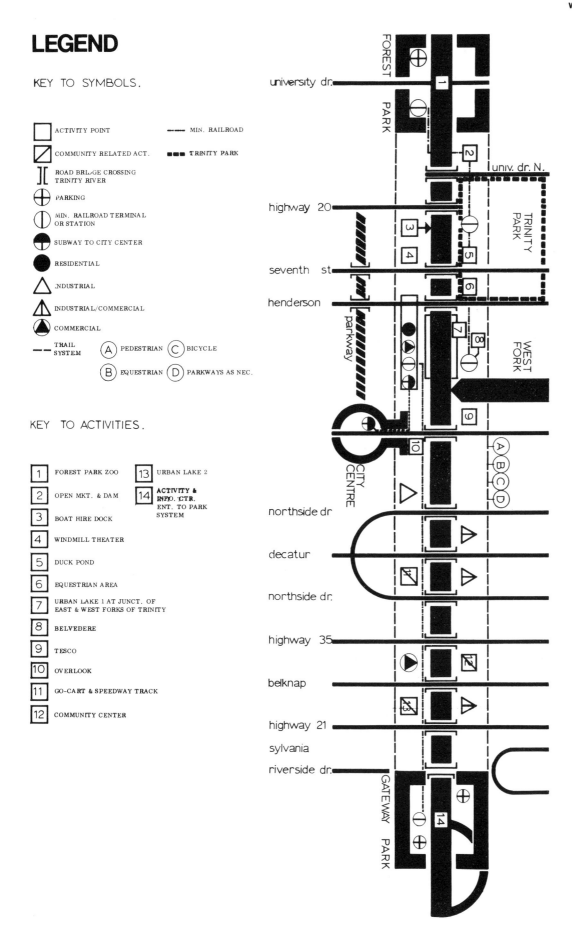

In a Take Part workshop for their downtown, people of Charlottesville, Virginia, performed scores together that helped them to plan their community for the future.

The Napa Valley Players act out one of the future planning options for Yountville at the annual Grange Banquet. The playlets were developed from scenario-scores prepared by Lawrence Halprin & Associates in response to recommendations from Take Part workshops for Yountville.

dimensional model for a future building or a maquette for a theatrical *mise-en-scène* would be contemporary equivalents. Recently, video-modeling experiments at the College of Environmental Design at the University of California, Berkeley, have been able to project the performance of various urban scores— that is, planning and development approaches—over time to show how they would affect San Francisco's downtown.

Since the workshops, "Experiments in Environment," scores and scoring have been instrumental for Halprin and colleagues in activating a number of processes that have expanded involvement and participation beyond the boundaries of the traditional creative process. The lessons learned in the 1966 and 1968 workshops gave rise to the conviction that people in communities could become important influences on how those communities evolve. Scoring activities that helped people to participate in hands-on design and planning situations produced impressive results in built environments. The first of these was in 1969 in Fort Worth, Texas, where a revived riverfront park system is its legacy. Later, downtown Charlottesville, Virginia, was in decline, victim of the suburban development and shopping-center malaise of many American communities. Residents, merchants, and representatives of city hall worked in community planning workshops with Lawrence Halprin & Associates to evolve plans and recommendations for saving the downtown area. That center is now redesigned and revitalized. The process of people's involvement in taking responsibility for their own environments came to be called Take Part[5]—at once its name and its definition. It has since been used in a number of different forms of collective creativity in addition to environmental design and planning.

Take Part processes, and the scores that activate them, can generally be characterized in two groupings: one toward the closed end of the score scale, and the other toward the open end. The former concerns situations that aim for one or more generally accepted objectives or expectations, sometimes in the form of projects to be built or community plans to be implemented. Because implementation is a major consideration, the overall process score tends to be somewhat specifically designed, with events and activities all focused toward the ultimate objective of realizing the plan or project. Within the overall score, there can be any number of more open sub-scores that will help people to rediscover their environments, collaborate on making designs and plans, and work together in creative ways toward a high level of agreement and understanding. Even within more closed, implementation-oriented scores, open scores can be effective. After people had participated in workshops to determine the future course of Yountville, a town in the California wine country, the alternative plans were demonstrated in the form of playlets acting out the consequences of each approach. Lawrence Halprin & Associates wrote loose scenarios for each, and they were then developed and acted out by the local theater troupe. It was a vivid way for people to understand the consequences of their proposals, and make informed decisions therefrom.

In these scored Take Part workshops, the designers of the scores also act as conductors of the process, comparable to the symphonic conductor of a score. They help people to enjoy themselves being creative, to keep the activity moving and not bog down in traditional adversarial situations of the "public meeting" or decision-by-voting, which always produces a group of losers. Appropriateness is the key to success in designing scores and Take Part processes. Having been burned enough times in the early applications of scores, Halprin and others pursuing this particular form of the *how* of creativity have learned to be sensitive both to the situation and to individuals, to try and uncover "hidden agendas" and use scores positively to help people participate. Scoring activities for people to perform implies a significant responsibility for maintaining respect and consideration for those people. Since scores, having no moral characteristics per se, can be used to manipulate and oppress people as much as to liberate them (consider Adolf Hitler and his closed score for the world), it behooves the designer and conductor of scores to deal respectfully with people's feelings. Scores as they are used in Take Part are to open people up to each other, to help vital energies flourish, to encourage explorations and agreements, to celebrate the positive resources of life and community and people.

Scoring, then, is deciding how to proceed, what activities will give appropriate directions and qualities to how people can work, play, create, live, and celebrate together. It is communicating the process to participants in forms that will help them to act. Scoring pertains, as well, to the solitary act of creativity during which the artist thinks through the process and then performs it to make art, the way a sketch or a plan precedes a painting or a garden. Some people, notably the artist Christo, have considered the activities and artifacts of scores and the creative process as much deserving of the appellation *art* as the final products themselves.

Scores give form to performance, and by doing so give performance many of its attributes. That is why it is vitally important to design the right scores for people and situations. A closed score for people who are bursting at the seams to get into energetic activities and express themselves might dampen all their enthusiasms. A score that is too open might alarm a group warily testing each other and their aims before deciding to proceed; it could stifle their tentative pushing into the process. An open score in a situation having dangerous social or political potentials may defeat its objectives by producing negative feelings among participants. A closed score that people feel only reinforces hierarchical patterns, which they already resent, would be equally negative.

The scores shown in this essay have a variety of qualities and intentions, explained in their captions. Some are closed and some are open; most have elements of both. They try to be direct and understandable, as well as evocative and interesting, so that people will want to do them. They have different reasons for being, different objectives. They also have a commonality—to involve people in some sort of shared activities, performances, and creativity. They are activators, goads, and guides. They help people traverse the *how* of creativity toward achieving its *what*.

Thirty-seven years after Larry Halprin wrote about designing gardens as a matrix to encourage people's activities, he, and through him many others, realizes that scores give form to the unique as well as to the quotidian—to grand garden designs and to your own vegetable patch, to *le grand cuisine* and to your daily grocery list, to grand opera and to "Row, Row, Row Your Boat." For about twenty years, the conscious exploration, experimentation, and practical applications of scores, and the performances of hundreds of scores, have enriched people's lives and helped them to enrich their own environments.

1. Lawrence Halprin, "The Choreography of Gardens," *Impulse*, San Francisco, 1949.

2. Ibid.

3. Note to Jim Burns from Lawrence Halprin, San Francisco, November 1985.

4. Suzanne, Duchess of St. Albans, "Ancient Magic," *Connoisseur*, November, 1985.

5. The process is called "Taking Part" by some workshop conductors and "Take Part" by others. The latter term is used in this essay.

"Le Pink Grapefruit" is a film about Salvador Dali created by Lawrence Halprin and Sue Yung Li Ikeda in RoundHouse (1975).

The Golden Voyage *by Douglas Davis*

DOUGLAS DAVIS *is an artist, writer and teacher. The architecture and design critic for* Newsweek, *he is the author of* Artculture: Essays in the Postmodern. *He has worked intensively in video, film, performance, drawing, and printmaking.*

Norm and "nature"... are always stressed in the critical discussions of classicists. Classic, by derivation, means exemplar or norm. Aristotle preferred a "probable impossible" (a technically impossible fact or act which represents the norm) to an "improbable possible" (a nonrepresentative fait accompli).... As [Alexander] Pope said, "Those rules of old, discovered, not devised, were nature still, but nature methodized."...

Because the wonderful is seen rationally as nonprobable, critical theory reacting against classicism may react against the probable. Men who seek novel experience and stress individual rights in ethics substitute the exploring of personal life for classical patterns of human experience. Art becomes subjective or "romantic" instead of objective or "classic."

Albert Cook, *The Dark Voyage and the Golden Mean,* 1966

Though he carries the bearded aura of romanticism, Lawrence Halprin is in fact the prime classicist of the American landscape, which includes the city. The overwhelmingly positive response to his parks, fountains, and plazas, wherever they are sited, is the final proof of this contention. In the purest Aristotelian sense, he has provided "norms" for all classes of people—that is, spaces for public (as opposed to private or subjective) enjoyment. It can be argued that the shapes, forms, and colors in these spaces result not just from him, but from a relentless attempt to involve the users in the original design process...that Halprin is not entirely responsible, in the manner of a single-minded Alexander Pope or Jean-Antoine Watteau, for what we see and experience in Ghirardelli Square, Lovejoy Plaza, or The Sea Ranch, to mention three of his best-known projects.

But, of course, the "norm" of one age cannot possibly duplicate the "norm" of another. The tiny elite that managed eighteenth-century high culture and high politics in Athens, Rome, or London is relatively impotent in Halprin's America, where millions of university-trained adults demand a share of the conceptual action

Above:
Ghirardelli Square, 1962,
San Francisco. View from San
Francisco Bay showing Ghirardelli,
in the mid-twenties, as an operat-
ing chocolate factory before its
conversion to a shopping complex.

Ghirardelli Square, 1962, San
Francisco. View from San Francisco Bay.

in politics, in the management of public schools and universities, in the funding of local museums—at a time when unprecedented advances in telecommunications and computer technology render instant, widely shared decision making easily possible. It is my contention that we still do not perceive the full implications of mass literacy and mass immediacy. Halprin does. His participative spaces respond to the meaning of our time as precisely as André Le Nôtre's rigidly ordered gardens at Versailles hymned the class structure of pre-revolutionary France, or the radical informality of John Nash's Regent's Park in nineteenth-century London announced (for those who would listen) the onset of a new democratic order.

Surely Halprin's impassioned followers will blanch to hear his name linked with Aristotle, with Pope, and most of all with Nash, in whose hands the loathed "Picturesque" tradition of landscape architecture came to life. For decades, Halprin has been lovingly cited by friends and critics alike in a rustic California role, along with many of his spaces. But this exhibition ought to inspire a larger vision of his work, placing it within the historical and international context where it belongs. We often forget that Halprin is a quintessentially urban spirit, informed as much by cities, by the Bauhaus tradition (he trained, after all, at Harvard in the Gropius era), as by the call of the wild. Like Richard Neutra, one of the first European émigrés in architecture to California, he informs everything he touches with a keen, well-educated, deeply referential sensibility. Perhaps no work of urban architecture since World War II has inspired a wider return to "the rules of old," as Pope would have put it, than Ghirardelli Square. Certainly no more cosmopolitan vision of his birthplace has ever been described than in his study, *New York New York*.

Ghirardelli Square, 1962, San Francisco. Ramps and balconies leading up to views of the Bay and Alcatraz Island.

Above:
Ghirardelli Square, 1962, San Francisco. Tiered platforms and courtyards.

Ghirardelli Square, 1962, San Francisco. An integrated plan of street furniture, paving, and fountains.

Notes on the Ghirardelli Center For Bill Roth

June '62

I's quite clear that much of the old brick stuff should stay — But some should come out !!!!

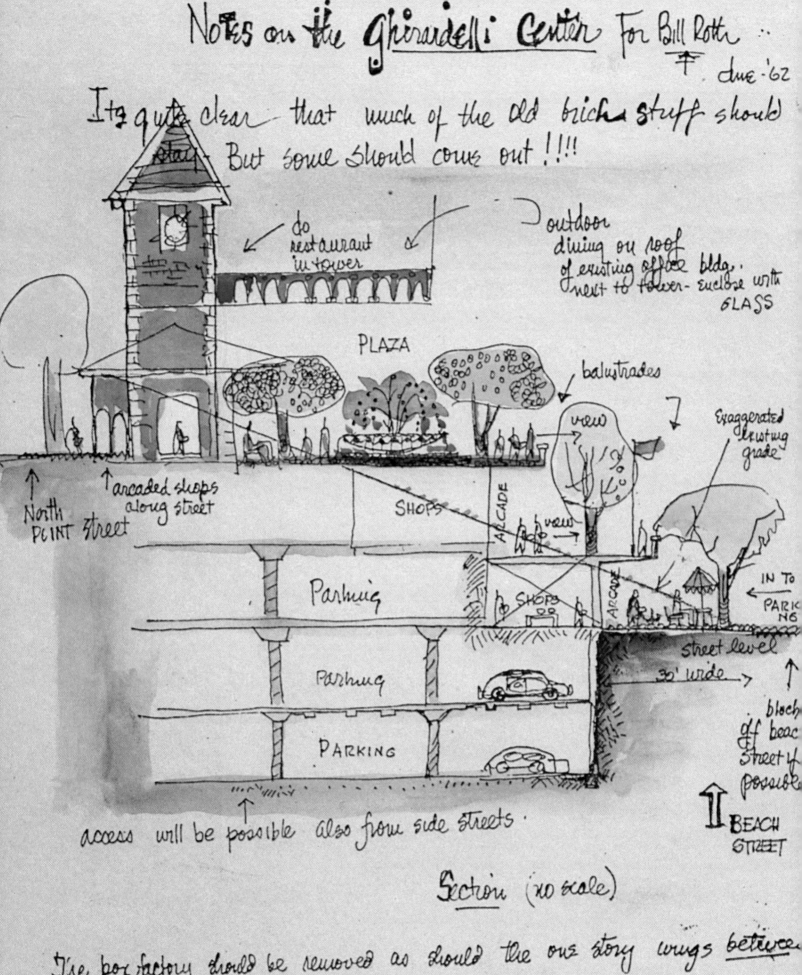

do restaurant in tower

Outdoor dining on roof of existing office bldg. next to tower - Enclose with GLASS

PLAZA

balustrades

view ?

North POINT Street

arcaded shops along street

SHOPS

ALCADE

view →

Exaggerated existing grade

do SHOPS

ARCADE

IN TO PARK ING

Parking

view →

street level

30' wide →

block of beac Street if possible

Parking

Parking

BEACH STREET

access will be possible also from side streets.

Section (no scale)

The box factory should be removed as should the one story wings between the old factories.

A great plaza at the upper level should be developed — around it a "BEEHIVE OF EXCITEMENT" with several

Indeed, the urban sensibility is often picturesque as a matter of self-defense: hemmed in by concrete, asphalt, and the freeway, its libido for warm, attractive, soothing places is fierce. Do not look for provocative, striking, unsettling imagery in the work of Lawrence Halprin. Find it in Philip Johnson or Marcel Breuer or in the metaphorical icons of the late Post-Modern style, in Michael Graves or Leon Krier—not in Halprin. Albert Cook argues in his brilliant analysis of the classic-romantic polarity that the classical poet is always searching for symbols that unite rather than divide, for the golden mean, in effect, while the romantic seeks to divide, to shock and conquer, to sail out alone on a dark voyage, seeking the improbable. A latter-day classicist, facing an "open" audience, Halprin combines these two polarities: he seeks the mean in flexible, reversible, arrangeable forms; his journey is golden, not dark, and it welcomes all of us, at once.

It is quite clear that much of the old brick stuff should stay. But some should come out!…A great plaza at the upper level should be developed—around it a BEEHIVE OF EXCITEMENT with several layers of shops, all connected with each other by ramps and stairs from different levels…. I think a motel—a very good one would be marvelous here—urban—urbane—lots of things to do—shopping, restaurants, an off-beat theater—avant-garde paintings and sculpture on the plaza—rotating exhibits— I'd come and stay for a weekend myself!

Lawrence Halprin, Notes on the Ghirardelli Center (for developer Bill Roth), 1965

We have forgotten in this revivalist decade—when there is barely one American city not attempting to rescue and preserve its aging downtown—how revolutionary was Halprin's design to save Ghirardelli in 1965. Granted it occured only one year before Robert Venturi published his *Complexity and Contradiction in Architecture*, and sentiment was just beginning to shift on campuses and in the younger design firms against the clean, antiseptic, "modern" approach to urban renewal, which insisted on blanket destruction of the old. The point is that Halprin acted effectively before anyone else. He conclusively proved that downtown can survive as DOWNTOWN, not as an imitation of a wide-open urban space.

A not so subtle irony in Halprin's work is that his preferred "landscape" is crowded, both with objects and people. I well recall my first visit to Ghirardelli with Halprin, not long after it opened. It was a bright, crowded weekend morning, the square jammed with people, and he spoke of nothing except the theater of movement going on all around us. "See that couple?" he said, pointing across the square. "Notice how they went up and down

Above:
Ghirardelli Square, 1962, San Francisco. East entrance.

Ghirardelli Square, 1962, San Francisco. Wall fountain.

Far left:
Ghirardelli Square, 1962, San Francisco. "Notes on the Ghirardelli Center," a drawing by Lawrence Halprin.

Seattle Freeway Park. View from Interstate 5.

Far right:
Seattle Freeway Park, 1970, Seattle. Waterfall.

Seattle Freeway Park, 1970, Seattle. Pathways.

that ramp, in a straight line, without thinking? You've got to choreograph movement like that." Though it is conventionally understood as a rural retreat, The Sea Ranch is clustered in the same manner, jamming most of the residents close together, offering them ramps, stairs, balconies, even in their backyards, around the swimming pools, celebrating— and directing—movement.

Halprin is one of those Sea Ranch residents, participating in its life as fully as he predicted to Bill Roth that he would at Ghirardelli. It is abundantly clear that Halprin choreographs not only the movements of others within his spaces but his own body as well. His personal commitment to what he does, his determination to enjoy what he builds sets him apart. But this personal involvement is hardly Byronic, hardly a Shelleyan soul on the loose. Halprin's deceptively casual free-hand sketches are in fact studies that probe for the norm in public behavior. Examine the drawings, before and after, for the Lovejoy Plaza in Portland, Oregon. Over and over you will find him prophesying or recording the gait of the people, the flow of the water, the wind in the trees. Yes, we know that these huge concrete forms are based on the study of nature, of waterfalls in the Sierra. What we actually see and experience in Portland is decidedly humanized, however, in the manner of Regent's Park: there are rectangles, spirals, steps, permitting freedom of movement formed by inclines, paths, ramps. The Seattle Freeway Park, piled high with massive concrete blocks, resembles a Parthenon of classical forms, each one smoothed and domesticated, finished off as a square or rectangle. Halprin's celebrated asymmetry is encircled by symmetry, or by memory. The magnificent fountain in San Francisco's Embarcadero Plaza, surely his funkiest, most ungainly work (executed in collaboration

with Armand Vaillancourt), is an assemblage of jutting, jagged forms that recalls nothing less than the bulldozing of the plaza itself. The material of the fountain is formed from an array of pipes, columns, and rubble left over when the destruction was completed. Even here, on the extreme of composition, Halprin touches a contemporary classical norm—decomposition itself.

Complexity, rather than simplicity, is a major factor in the process of making cities exciting and interesting and therefore satisfying places to live. One of our criticisms of much of the redevelopment projects that have been built over the last decades is that, because of their extreme simplicity and lack of variety of facilities and uses, they are sterile and dull and therefore uninteresting places to be in.

Lawrence Halprin, *New York New York*, 1968

Halprin's *New York New York* is easily the least-known work of excellence in urban planning in our time. It antedated the recent obsession with mixed-use condominiums, street malls, and plazas. It predicted the surge in the popularity of tiny vest-pocket parks in New York as well as the hatred for the automobile (which recently doomed Manhattan's otherwise benign Westway system of parks and highways). Halprin's study, based on six sites in New York—and a battery of interviews with city residents—argues, again and again, against the mindless imposition of "open" spaces in dense, crowded city spaces. It correctly sees the city as an excuse to enjoy many options, rather than just a few: privacy, company, work, play, smallness, bigness, activity, repose, tension, relaxation. More importantly, *New York New York* pays the citizen the unaccustomed compliment of assuming that he desires a multiplicity of these options—in brief, that he is human. How striking is the contrast between *New York New York* and virtually all other attempts to plan and revamp large public areas, whether urban or rural, from Pierre L'Enfant to Le Corbusier to the latest master plan endorsed by your city or neighborhood developer. But *New York New York* is based on the solid reality of our time, of 250 million post-industrial Americans, most of them relatively affluent, demanding, shifting, mobile, and with a limitless appetite for experience of all kinds.

Embarcadero Plaza and Fountain (now M. Justin Herman Plaza), 1962, San Francisco. Vaillancourt Fountain with the Ferry Building in the background behind elevated freeway.

We have been searching for archetypal relationships—in workshops which take place primarily out in the field. These TAKING PART workshops allow people the opportunity to discover and articulate their own needs and desires for themselves and for their communities.

Lawrence Halprin, *Process Architecture,* No. 4, 1977

The drive back and down to the archetype, doubtless inspired by his wife Anna's extraordinary dance workshops in the mid-1960s, has become one of Lawrence Halprin's main goals in recent years. The persistence of basic geometry in all his work, the recurrent use of the tree, of flowing water, are all examples. That they emerge over and over from each of his workshops and projects is no criticism of his intention to share creativity. Surely the result of any intensely collaborative exercise is a symbol based in common understanding.

Though the Franklin Delano Roosevelt Memorial in Washington, D.C., did not emerge from a Taking Part workshop, it displays many characteristics of one that might have, offering a multiplicity of options along a continuous, winding wall, including smells, sounds, lights, newsreel footage, relief sculpture, and, of course, constant access to the sound and rhythm of running water. Though the memorial is unfinished as I write, my instinct is that it will become the central achievement of Halprin's career, for reasons far beyond the simply physical or formal. In its serial complexity, the FDR project defines more than the multifaceted nature of Roosevelt himself. It allows the visitor to focus on now this, now that aspect of a president whose inauguration closed off one version of the American dream and opened up another, still embattled, still under siege. Not far away, the grand but closed and self-defined figures reared to honor Lincoln, Jefferson, and Washington stand in poignant contrast. Though they are normally considered "classical," though Halprin is widely regarded as a nouveau-riche interloper into our Arcadian capital city, I am arguing that the reverse is true: he is offering a golden mean to an audience for whom participation in a multiplicity of viewpoints and interpretations is "natural," while the solitary, competing figures are not. By voyaging along this winding wall that flanks the Potomac River, each person will discover his own truth, without presuming that it precludes the others. In this critical site, therefore, at the crossroads of Halprin's career, the FDR Memorial gives voice to an unspoken consensus about how we intend increasingly to govern ourselves.

Embarcadero Plaza and Fountain (now M. Justin Herman Plaza), 1962, San Francisco. In the Vaillancourt Fountain.

Psychology and the Roots of Design
by Dr. Joseph L. Henderson

DR. JOSEPH L. HENDERSON, *an
eminent analytical psychologist,
trained in Zurich with Carl Jung in
the 1930s. Dr. Henderson has been in
private practice since 1938 and is a
founding member and teacher at the
C.G. Jung Institute in San Francisco.
He is the author of "Ancient Myths and
Modern Man" in* Man and His
Symbols, *edited by C.G. Jung (1964),*
Threshholds of Initiation *(1967), and*
Cultural Attitudes in Psychological
Perspective *(1984).*

Modern depth psychology and anthro-
pology, especially associated with the names
of C.G. Jung, Mircea Eliade, Claude Levi-
Strauss, and the original Gestalt psychologists,
have described the imaginative function of the
human psyche as being able to produce
spontaneous images that cannot result from
sensory perceptions alone. We usually call
them archetypal images because they have no
antecedents and emerge from the unconscious
as preformed abstractions. From my study of
dreams, I would categorize these images as of
two different types.

The first type is a centered image; and the
second, an image of liberated movement.
The centered image may have a formative
influence in the design of houses, temples,
tombs, formal gardens, amphitheaters, and
public spaces. The other image is associated
with linear progressions and is found in
walkways, bridges, towers, tunnels, stairways,
and various labyrinthian passages. The
centered designs have a fixed point from
which everything else is placed at a suitable
distance. The linear design, on the other hand,
always moves beyond any fixed points in
the search for new and different levels of
experience. The landscape architecture of

Lawrence Halprin utilizes this linear image in
a consistent yet flexible way. For me his
designs seem to depend on the creation of a
moving line as an ordering principle by which
people can experience nature archetypally.

In his introduction to *The Sketchbooks of
Lawrence Halprin,* Jim Burns expresses this
very well by saying: "… nature, people, and
the designer aspire toward a seamless 'whole'
in environmental creativity. As there is an
ecology of successional forms in nature, there
is—or can be—an evolution of cultural forms
in human society."[1] I am suggesting that the
basic image for this evolutionary activity is as
inwardly creative as the activity of the DNA
molecule when visualized by biologists as a
moving series of linear forms that are open-
ended, never to be perfected or finalized.
Burns senses this in relation to Halprin's work
when he says the moving line becomes a
"metaphor for process-activity."[2]

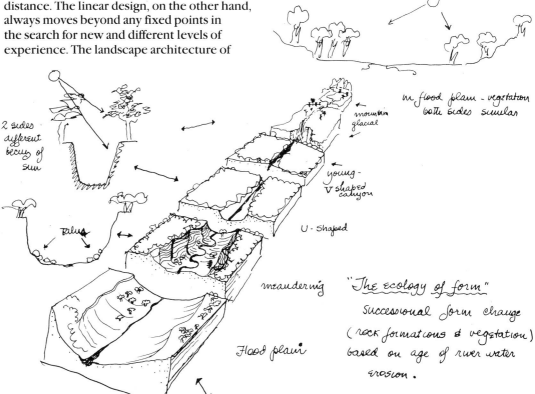

**Drawing by Lawrence Halprin from
his notebooks.**

The city of Jerusalem depicting a minaret as example of a linear archetypal image. A drawing by Lawrence Halprin from his notebooks.

Below:
Aerial view of the Bighorn Medicine Wheel in Wyoming as example of a centered archetypal image.

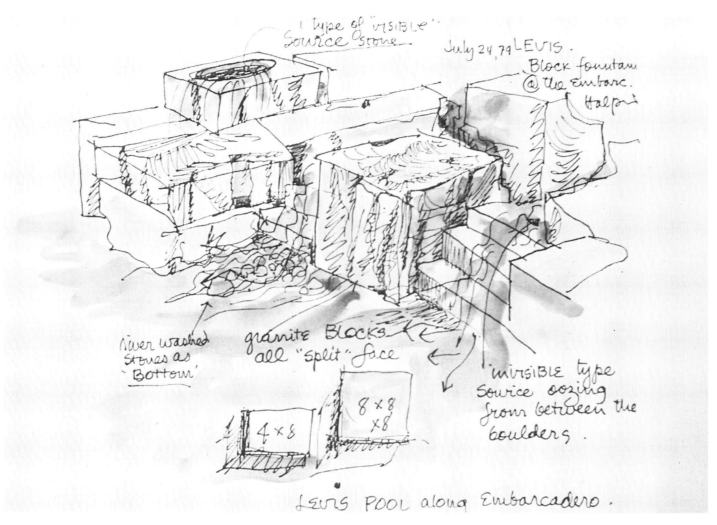

(handwritten sketch annotations):

1 type of "visible" Source Stone.

July 24, 79 LEVIS. Block fountain @ the Embarc. Halprin

River washed stones as "Bottom"

granite BLOCKS all "split" face

4 × 8

8 × 8 × 8

"invisible type Source oozing from between the boulders.

LEVIS POOL along Embarcadero.

Levi's Plaza, 1978, San Francisco. Levi's stream. Drawing by Lawrence Halprin.

Above: Levi's Plaza, 1978, San Francisco. Levi's pool along The Embarcadero.

Bringing this metaphor into specific focus, we find how many different forms this basic linear pattern may take as to whether it is straight, vertical, curvilinear, horizontal, or meandering. Halprin's Levi's Plaza in San Francisco perhaps most perfectly realizes his concept of centering through movement. Levi's pool is the "experiential equivalent" of a mountain waterfall, but it is then made to flow down to form Levi's stream as it pursues a meandering course through green parklike mounds of grass that will "insulate people from the outside world…its noise and cacophony." It is a quite magical device in providing a sense of rural peace and quiet, so close to the San Francisco embarcadero and its freeway, with the vertical thrust of Telegraph Hill and Coit Tower behind. A small view of the bay from the plaza also ensures that we know that Levi's stream, which evokes such an experience of mountain heights, will reach the sea where its course is completed.

In our stroll, we have come from the Sierra down to the sea as an "experiential equivalent" of the whole California landscape—but our stroll through this park may do more than relate us to nature or the California landscape. A synthesis of human experience and nature inevitably activates the inner image of the moving line that unites height with depth. The inner image of this movement does more. It evokes an inborn psychological need for change embodied in the archetypal predisposition that we all have to take a journey with the

Above:
Levi's Plaza, 1978, San Francisco. The large granite rock in the more urban-like setting of the park comes from the foothills of the High Sierra.

Levi's Plaza, 1978, San Francisco. The symbolism of the meandering stream and water-washed rocks reflects on the origins of Levi Strauss during California's gold rush.

is a re-building of the last destroyed portion of the ancient Jewish quarter... called the ROVAH.

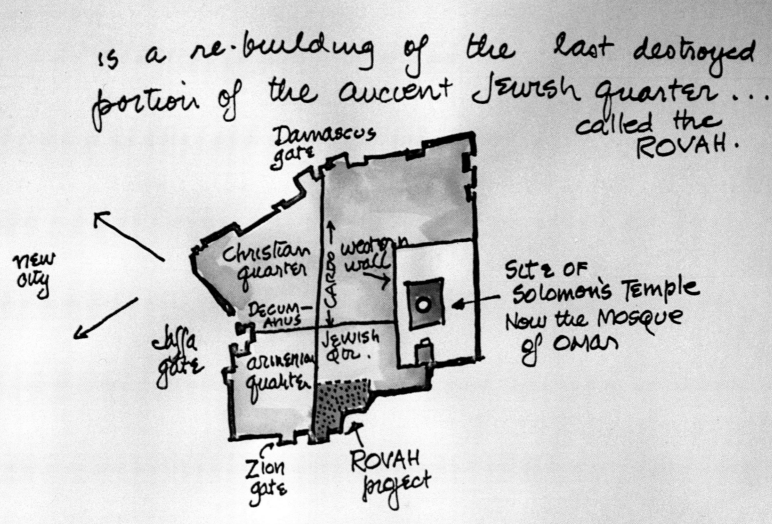

I have searched for ways to stay with the grain character & scale of the ancient city in rebuilding it. and to insert modern living facilities: underground parking, new housing - while at the same time preserving the ancient newly excavated Byzantine churches, roads & Biblical artifacts to make an archaeological garden.
....
The second project stretching from the ridge line of the United Nations Headqrts overlooking the city 2 kilometers away involves a kind of regional preservation based on aesthetic as well as ecological

promise of an adventure of self-discovery.

For many people this kind of adventure may not include a new experience of nature, but an old experience of history. Here, Halprin's designs for his Jerusalem projects come to mind. One of these is a rebuilding of the last destroyed portion of the ancient Jewish Quarter called the Rovah, inside the Old City wall. "I have searched for ways to stay with the grain, character, and scale of the ancient city in rebuilding it. And to insert modern living facilities…at the same time preserving the ancient, newly excavated Byzantine churches …to make an archeological garden." In contrast to being out in nature, here Halprin is back in history in a way that suggests we might view the past with interior vision— psychologically as well as esthetically. This recalls Kenneth Clark's descriptions of art as existing not just for its own sake, but as a vehicle for understanding better the people who made the art and the time that made them. I find the need for this view of history frequently in my patients. They do not need the facts of history so much as the sense that they are the products of a long historical process. The "history," indeed, is like an archeological garden since the makers of history could never have dreamed how it would look until it was more or less completed. To put it another way, what we are really hoping to find in the past can only be revealed in the light of the future.

Above:
The Rovah Buildings and Garden, 1980, Jerusalem. Model of overall site showing bus terminal, parking gargage, housing, cafés, and an archeological garden.

The Rovah Buildings and Garden, 1980, Jerusalem. Model of entrance tunnel under the Old City wall designed to meet the modern needs of the city, while preserving its past.

Far left:
The Old City of Jerusalem. A drawing by Lawrence Halprin from his notebooks.

**Walter and Elise Haas Promenade,
1984, Jerusalem. View of the promenade from a ridge overlooking
Jerusalem. Drawing by Lawrence
Halprin.**

Another of Halprin's projects in Jerusalem
takes him more into his true field as a landscape architect. Here he designs a promenade
overlooking the city two kilometers away as
a kind of "regional preservation based on
esthetic as well as ecological principles...to
maintain its Biblical landscape with its small
network of villages...to preserve this ancient
landscape while allowing organic change to
occur and to encourage people's participation
and enjoyment." Again we recognize the

theme of the journey, but this time it is
historically oriented. It recalls a past that may
be re-created by knowledge of the present and
anticipation of its own future for the people
living in this area. It is an experience that
Halprin is especially capable of providing,
since his involvement with Jerusalem goes
back many years and continues today to
profoundly affect his life and attitudes.

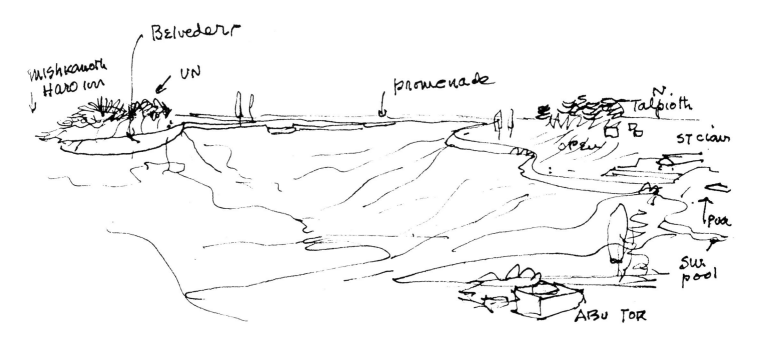

12. ARMON HANATZIV AREA.
PROMENADE · OVERLOOK · PICNIC AREAS etc.
June 1971

Below:
Lifta, 1985, Israel. Inhabited since Biblical times, this village, at the northern edge of Jerusalem, is being restored as a nature reserve and study center.

Holocaust Memorial Competition, 1982, San Francisco. A drawing by Lawrence Halprin.

A particularly dramatic use of the linear image is found in Halprin's proposed design for the Holocaust Memorial for the plaza in front of the California Palace of the Legion of Honor in San Francisco. He had the vision of a spiral ramp that would carry visitors in a circular journey toward an inner center, which, suddenly, at its point of greatest constriction, opens into a tunnel that leads to a view of the Golden Gate Bridge with its suggestion of liberated movement. This also could symbolize a significant rite of passage by which linear movement through space could help people relive and yet experience a healing ritual for the greatest human tragedy of modern times.

From descriptions of these particular projects, one might tend to regard Halprin as having a cultural attitude that combines both religious and esthetic sensitivity. Knowing him personally, as a friend of long standing, I do think this characterizes his main creative motivation. There is another cultural attitude, however, that appears at significant moments in his life and work. It is what I would call a social attitude, but it is not based on any intellectual system of ideas nor is it a call for social action. Perhaps it can be best understood as a social judgment—an appreciation of those humanisitc values that are eternally true, if they are true at all.

The really striking example of Halprin's sensitivity to social values is found in the Franklin Delano Roosevelt Memorial in Washington, D.C. Of it he says: "The great views out to the 3 memorials to Lincoln, Jefferson and Washington and across the Tidal Basin link FDR to monumental Washington. Sculpture in the memorial is to

Holocaust Memorial Competition, 1982, San Francisco. A spiral plan is used to lead visitors down a ramp in a simulated experience of incarceration. Drawing by Lawrence Halprin.

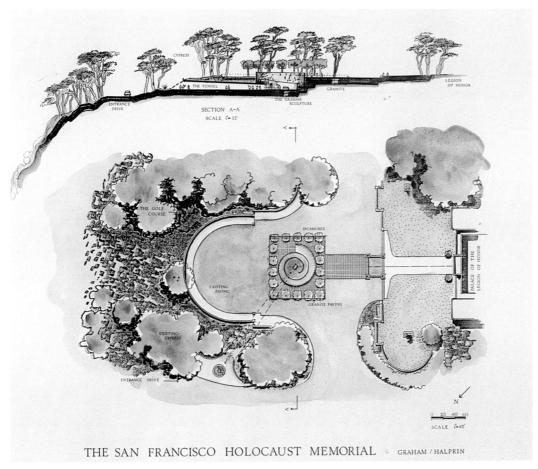

Holocaust Memorial Competition, 1982, San Francisco. Plan and elevation.

Franklin Delano Roosevelt Memorial, 1976, Washington, D.C. Water is a major theme throughout the plan, as it was in Roosevelt's life. Model made for the *Franklin Delano Roosevelt Memorial* film by Glen Fleck.

personalize ... and articulate the events of FDR's times—so critical to our country. It is conceived as a long frieze of reliefs on and in the wall ... with the carved great quotations which did so much to mobilize the feelings and attitudes of the people ... during his lifetime as president." It is to FDR's own social attitude that Halprin clearly responds. Roosevelt was brought up to obey the psychological attitude of noblesse oblige and was trained from early boyhood by his father and at Groton School, under the influence of Endicott Peabody, to place the advantages of his upbringing and education in service to mankind ... that he was non-intellectual but learned "by osmosis" from people.

These descriptions point to the personality of a man with strong extraverted intuition allied with feeling, which of all psychological functions opens the way to easy social interaction. But, it also opens such a person to violent criticism when such humanitarianism moves traditional people to change their accustomed views or modes of life radically. The time of the 1930s and 1940s in America was such a time of stress and a time of transition on so many levels that established customs were unsettled by it. It becomes of special interest to see how Halprin asks us to pause, re-evaluate, and appreciate this period by his design for the memorial.

Here also the linear design predominates, but instead of suggesting a long journey of fresh discovery it is constructed to allow us to observe a specific series of "experiential equivalents" of the life of a man and his impact upon the period during which he lived. Halprin has, therefore, provided the memorial with "a series of processional spaces ... [with] 4 major outdoor rooms as spaces connected by 3 garden passageways which are narrower! The 4 rooms express the 4 freedoms, the 4 great sections of the country and 4 facets of the life cycle." To me this allegorical description could well be extended to include a sense of the archetypal significance of the number four symbolizing wholeness, as these formed spaces punctuate the linear design in a particularly meaningful way.

The movement of history is well represented by an image of the processional with significant stopping places for reorientation along the way. The three processional garden passageways accomplish this purpose to perfection since three always represents movement and four represents stability and focus. We cannot, of course, tell how this movement and its resting places will be experienced when the memorial is built, but I like to imagine that it may activate a deeper memory of something that precedes history altogether like primitive rites of passage that mark initiation rites of death and renewal in sacred caves, tombs, and temples of the distant past.

The difference between such ancient artifacts and Halprin's designs is that instead of the closed and secret spaces of ancient religious practices we find here a truly American, democratic, twentieth-century feeling of openness and respect for the environment with care for preservation of nature. Just as Halprin is able to block out traffic noises in the recesses of Levi's Plaza, so here at the Roosevelt Memorial he uses falling water that "will serve as white sound to mask the jet noise from the National Airport." And so, in many ways (some obvious and others as subtle as this) we are introduced to a natural world composed of air, water, and earth in artistic combination for the use of human beings who can stop long enough in their movements to remember from whence they have come as well as where they may be going.

1. *The Sketchbooks of Lawrence Halprin*, Process Architecture, Tokyo, Japan, 1981, 14.

2. All quoted material, here and following, comes from Lawrence Halprin's personal notebooks.

The Client's View *by Robert F. Maguire III*

ROBERT F. MAGUIRE III *is the co-founder of Maguire Thomas Partners, a major southern California investment builder. Influenced by Maguire's strong interest in urban planning and architecture, the firm has worked with internationally recognized architects such as Frank O. Gehry, Philip Johnson, and Cesar Pelli and is noted for the architectural distinction of its projects. Maguire's interest in the quality of urban life has also led to his involvement with groups such as the Aspen Institute, the Nature Conservancy, and the Dean's Council of the School of Architecture and Planning, University of California, Los Angeles.*

Although I had known of Larry Halprin's work for many years and appreciated it deeply, our professional relationship began about eight years ago when Harvey Perloff, the late dean of the School of Architecture and Urban Planning at the University of California, Los Angeles, and I put together the team for the Bunker Hill competition in Los Angeles. The team was comprised of Lawrence Halprin, Charles Moore, Barton Myers, Cesar Pelli, Ricardo Legorreta, Frank O. Gehry, Hugh Hardy, Robert Kennard, and others.

The team's goal was to devise a plan to transform the heart of Los Angeles from a stark urban renewal plot into a place of delight and humanity. We created great things but lamentably we lost the competition; an event that had little to do with the talent of the team but much to do with our political inexperience. Larry and Charles gave the inspiration for an enchanting series of great and varied public spaces. We all worked together as a team with great exuberance, laughter, and purpose but most of all with the instinct that we were creating something utterly unique.

That experience — from the joy of creation to the anguish of defeat — forged a special relationship between Larry and me. We have since marched on together in the stimulating

Bunker Hill Competition, 1980, Los Angeles. Perspective of Second Avenue courtyard. Drawing by Lawrence Halprin.

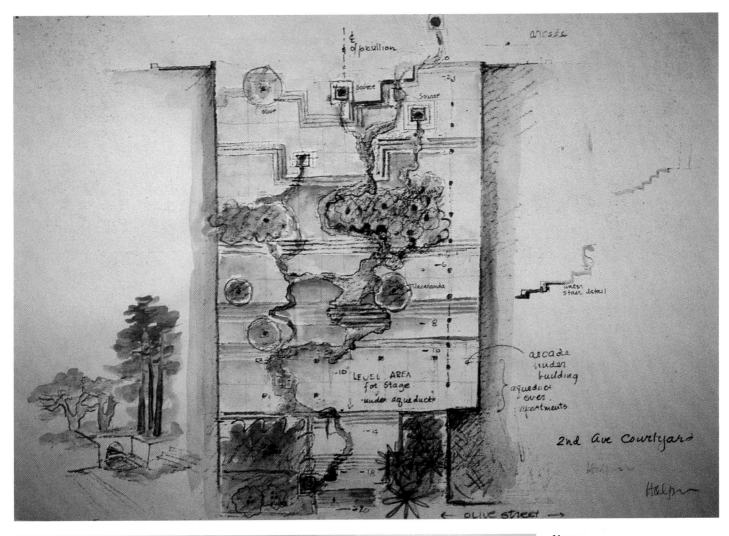

Above:
Bunker Hill Competition,
1980, Los Angeles. Plan of Second
Avenue courtyard. Drawing
by Lawrence Halprin.

Bunker Hill Competition, 1980.
Los Angeles. Water-stair courtyard.
Drawing by Lawrence Halprin.

Above:
Bunker Hill Steps, 1982,
Los Angeles. Earliest study model
of fountain.

Bunker Hill Steps, 1982,
Los Angeles. Later study model
of fountain.

Bunker Hill Steps, 1982,
Los Angeles. Most recent study
model of fountain.

**Bunker Hill Steps, 1982,
Los Angeles. View of stairs from
Fifth Street. Model.**

battle to make cities better. Larry and Charles are collaborating again on our Plaza Las Fuentes project in Pasadena, California, creating a beautiful public space. This is a project that will be built.

Larry and I are currently working together on Library Square, a project of such financial complexity as to deaden the minds of us all — particularly me — but one of great promise to the city of Los Angeles. The team, comprised of Larry, Harry Cobb, Barton Myers, and the late Harvey Perloff, made a plan of giant proportions. In bold moves, we anchored the center of downtown Los Angeles irreversibly, creating two marvelous buildings, and are saving and expanding Bertram Goodhue's Los Angeles Central Library. Also included in the project is a beautiful new park with provisions for a museum and the Bunker Hill Steps. Both the park and the steps are designed by Larry. The latter will link downtown Los Angeles to Bunker Hill in what will be the best public space this side of anywhere and clearly the best in Los Angeles.

Nearby, Larry collaborated with Marc Goldstein of Skidmore, Owings & Merrill and the sculptor Robert Graham to create Crocker

Above:
Plaza Las Fuentes, 1982, Pasadena, California. Model of central fountain. With Moore, Ruble & Yudell.

Library Gardens, 1982, Los Angeles.

Far right:
Bunker Hill Steps, 1982, Los Angeles. Aerial view of stairs. Model.

Crocker Court, 1981, Los Angeles.
Drawing by Lawrence Halprin of
atrium plantings.

Robert Maguire, Robert Graham (sitting),
and Lawrence Halprin in Crocker Court.

Court as a place of serenity and beauty in our
Crocker Center project in downtown Los
Angeles.

Our relationship is intricate since, although
I am the client and Larry the artist, I like to
be involved in the design effort. Larry has
great affection for me and makes large
allowances to accommodate my contradictory
lunges because he knows I share his will to
create memorable spaces. I, together with my
wife Sue, am committed to a deep involvement
in the creative process, encouraging the artists
and architects, while balancing on the tight
rope of giving support without invading the
artist's realm.

Larry has a deep wisdom and openness
gained over his nearly seventy years and has
come to grips with the uncertainty and doubt
involved in creativity. I haven't completely,
and he supports my efforts with great caring. I
suppose I give him similar support by offering
him interesting opportunities to work his great
artistry — and, through all of this, we remain
fast friends and collaborators.

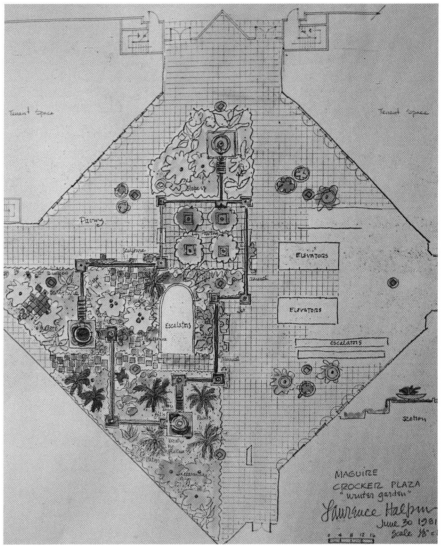

Crocker Court, 1981, Los Angeles.
Drawing by Lawrence Halprin of
atrium plan.

Far left:
Crocker Court, 1981, Los Angeles.
Sculpture by Robert Graham.

The Franklin Delano Roosevelt Memorial *by Phyllis Tuchman*

PHYLLIS TUCHMAN, *critic, curator, and teacher has written numerous articles, interviews, and exhibition catalogs for* Artforum, Art in America, Architectural Digest, *and* Newsday. *She received a NEA Art Critics Grant in 1978-79, and was a NEH fellow at Princeton University, Princeton, New Jersey, 1980. Tuchman has organized a number of exhibitions on contemporary sculpture including* Six in Bronze, *Williams College Museum of Art, Williamstown, Massachusetts, 1984, and is the author of* George Segal *(1983). She has taught at Hunter College, City University of New York, and Williams College, Williamstown.*

Lawrence Halprin's plans for the Franklin Delano Roosevelt Memorial will transform a sixty-six-acre site along the Tidal Basin in Washington, D.C., into a series of outdoor rooms featuring aspects of the life and times of the 32nd president of the United States. A sequence of spaces, structured by a meandering 800-foot-long, 14-foot-high rusticated granite wall, will include bas-reliefs and sculptures of people and events from the 1930s and 1940s, by such sculptors as Leonard Baskin, Neil Estern, Robert Graham, and George Segal. On the wall and on benches along a broad granite path, calligrapher John Benson will carve quotations from Roosevelt's official addresses, informal radio broadcasts, and speeches from his four national campaigns. Shrubs, flowers, ferns, grasses, ground coverings, and vines will be planted among already existing elms that will lead toward the famous Japanese cherry trees on the perimeter. All sorts of water play such as tranquil pools, rivulets in runnels, and a climactic group of falls cascading over the last section of stone blocks will also be prominent.

Halprin's blend of fine arts with landscape elements represents a sensitive reconsideration of the nature of monuments without deviating from the kind of old-fashioned ideals embodied in such projects. Halprin always felt, as he indicated on a sheet of notes early on, that the FDR Memorial "must be serious but not solemn." He envisioned a place readily accessible and emotionally evocative to the public without having to rely upon, as he said recently, "a great structure or something else that was awesome." In a city identified by neoclassical monuments, he sought to create "a spatial experience in the landscape." According to Halprin, "all the great archetypal memorials…are based on a series of progressions." Aspects of the future FDR Memorial are shared in common with the Ise Shrine in Japan, the complex at Karnak in Egypt, the Athenian Acropolis, the Inner City of Peking, and, in modern times, Erik Gunnar Asplund's Crematorium in Stockholm.

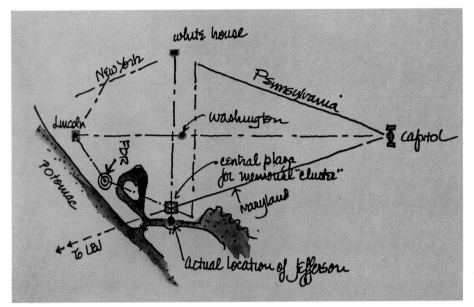

The Kite Plan was devised by the McMillian Commission in 1901 to reunify what had once been the master plan of Washington, D.C. The Roosevelt Memorial will be sited between the Jefferson and Lincoln memorials.

Below:
Franklin Delano Roosevelt Memorial, 1976, Washington, D.C. Model made for *The Franklin Delano Roosevelt Memorial* film by Glen Fleck.

Franklin Delano Roosevelt Memorial, 1976, Washington, D.C. A series of scores investigating issues of light, sound, and movement in and around the memorial. Drawing by Lawrence Halprin.

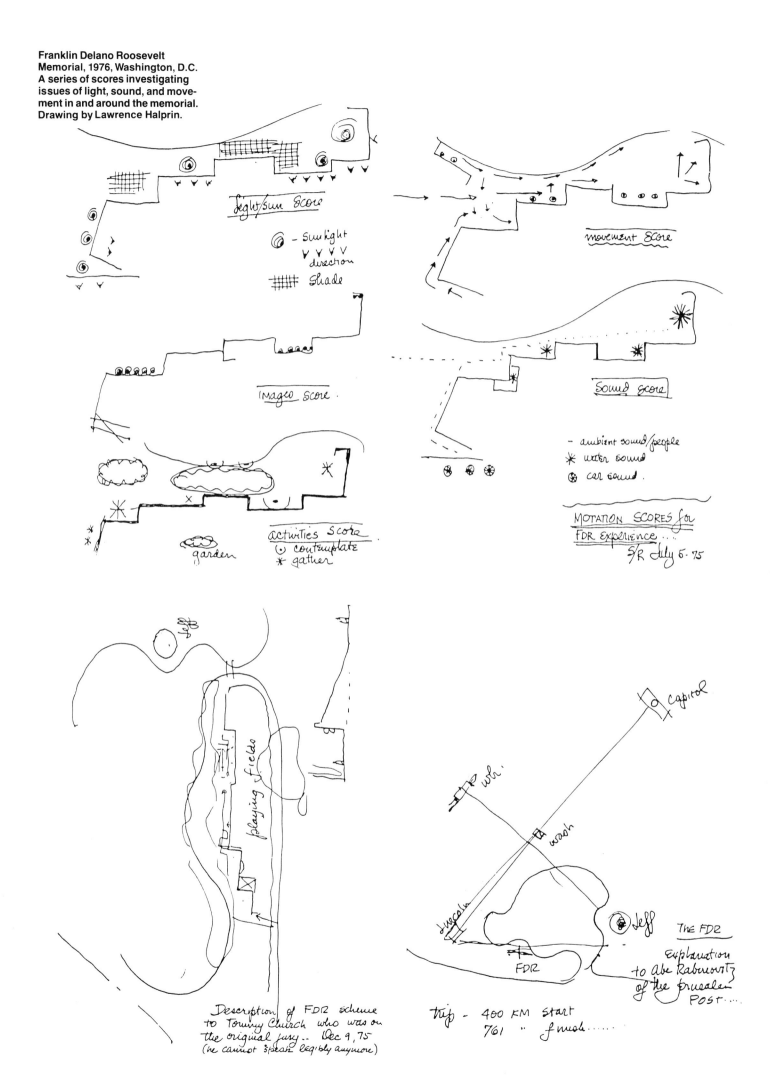

light/sun Score

⊚ – sunlight
∨ ∨ ∨ ∨ direction
▦ shade

movement score

imaged score .

sound score

activities score .
⊙ contemplate
✳ gather
garden

– ambient sound/people
✳ water sound
⊛ car sound .

MOTATION SCORES for
FDR EXPERIENCE ...
S/R July 5 · 75

playing fields
left

Description of FDR scheme
to Tommy Church who was on
the original jury .. Dec 9, 75
(he cannot speak legibly anymore)

capitol
wh.
wash
lincoln
FDR
⊚ Jeff

THE FDR
Explanation
to Abe Rabinowitz
of the Jerusalem
Post....

trip – 400 KM start
761 " finish......

Halprin first visited West Potomac Park in September 1971 at the request of former Governor Edmund G. Brown of California and with the endorsement of Senator Mark O. Hatfield of Oregon. Both men were familiar with Halprin's civic projects in the San Francisco Bay Area, Portland, Oregon, and Seattle. Halprin returned to Washington, D.C., for another look in March 1974. At that time he was already interested in generating a range of feelings from the public "as they approached [the memorial], as they are in it, as they look out of it, [and] as they remember it after they have left." The task would not be easy. During his second trip to the capital, the landscape architect observed, "The *site* is '*very* difficult' because it is so negative." He noted additionally, "It is long and flat with a slight camber in the center and has no sense of place." Nevertheless, Halprin had some notion about how he could achieve "a kind of built-in meditation." Two months later, he was invited by the Franklin Delano Roosevelt Commission, a panel composed of United States senators, representatives, and civilians to design the memorial.

Halprin was asked to proceed where others before him had failed. Congress first passed a resolution to establish a commission to investigate the possibilities for a memorial to FDR in 1946, a year after the president died. The commission finally was established in 1955, and four years later the site in West Potomac Park was set aside for the project. This tract of land runs along one segment of the so-called "kite plan" devised by the McMillan Commission in 1901 to reunify what had once been the master plan of the capital. The underlying geometry of the city needed to be revamped to accommodate new focal points on landfill reclaimed from marshy Potomac flats. The FDR Memorial will be located on one of the two sections of the "kite" that connect the Lincoln and Jefferson memorials.

In December 1960, New York architects William Pederson and Bradford Tilney were selected from among 547 competition entries to design the memorial to FDR. Thirteen months later the FDR Memorial Commission approved their proposal for eight concrete stelas inscribed with quotations, but the Commission of Fine Arts rejected the same renderings soon afterward. Although both groups accepted Pederson and Tilney's revised plans in 1964, they were abandoned the following spring. Then, in January 1966, after a review of fifty-five architects, Marcel Breuer was asked to create the memorial. The FDR Commission okayed Breuer's proposal that December to install a thirty-two-foot cube of polished stone with an incised portrait of the president and surround it with seven tall, rough granite slabs. The Commission of Fine Arts turned this plan down the following month. Two years later President Lyndon Johnson designated twenty-seven acres of

Franklin Delano Roosevelt Memorial, 1976, Washington, D.C. Drawing by Lawrence Halprin.

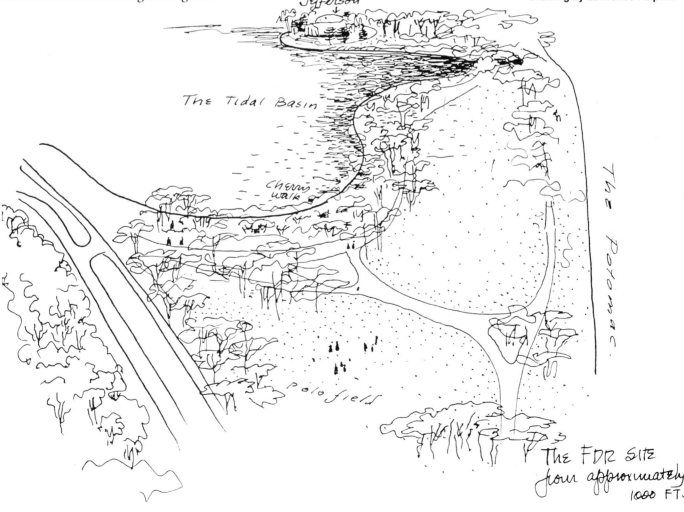

West Potomac Park to be developed as a rose garden known as the FDR Memorial Park. Eventually Lawrence Halprin was appointed designer for a more ambitious memorial on the site that would have been this park. Halprin's plans have been approved by every conceivable committee, and the commission merely awaits the appropriation of funds before breaking ground.

Memorials to presidents often take years to come to fruition. Robert Mills designed the Washington Monument in 1833. Yet construction did not begin until 1848. After work was interrupted by the Civil War, the monument finally was dedicated in 1884. A decade and a half passed before the Jefferson Memorial was completed. Resolutions for a fitting monument to the 3rd president were introduced by a Tammany Hall politician at the beginning of a series of sessions of the House of Representatives and were tabled until the Seventy-third Congress took action. A commission was established in April 1935 and John Russell Pope, the newly appointed architect for the National Gallery of Art on the mall, was named to design the Jefferson Memorial during the winter of 1937. His plans were not embraced wholeheartedly. According to "Basin Battle," an article in the 19 April 1937 issue of *Time*, "the extremely vocal opponents...included: modernist artists, objecting to the arid classicism of the scheme; Republicans and conservatives eager to spike this glorification of the Democratic Party;

garden club members, fearing the threat to the cherry trees; utilitarians who favor a memorial to Thomas Jefferson but favor something of public use, specifically an auditorium where such ceremonies as a Presidential inauguration may be held in weather like that of the last one." Today the enchanting nature of the Jefferson Memorial is unquestioned, but in 1937 the *Washington Post* argued, "A terrain world famous for its beauty would become a replica of a mining camp. A decade would scarcely suffice to restore its present charm."

Halprin would like the FDR Memorial to be the kind of place people visit repeatedly. They could return again and again the way they go to a museum to reacquaint themselves with the old master collections rather than the special exhibitions. Sculptor Robert Graham has expressed similar views and has mentioned the "resonance of emotions" that families can share. Graham, for example, has pointed out that memorials are not about the latest trends in the art world. Rather, they can engender "a beautiful, moving, gripping experience [which] has nothing to do with whether a work sells or if art magazines like it."

The FDR Memorial will not dominate the skyline of Washington, D.C., the way other monuments do. As you approach West Potomac Park you might even suspect it's not there. That is because a berm will separate it from the athletic fields Halprin was asked to retain. (He has referred to the much-used baseball diamonds as a "secular" area opposed

In one of the 4 "garden room" spaces · FDR memorial on Washington's birthday

Franklin Delano Roosevelt Memorial, 1976, Washington, D.C. A profile study of Roosevelt planned as a wall relief. By Leonard Baskin.

Far right:
**Franklin Delano Roosevelt Memorial, 1976, Washington, D.C. A Sequence of four rooms in the memorial symbolic of the four freedoms, the four terms of Roosevelt's presidency, and the four regional sections of the United States.
Drawing by Lawrence Halprin.**

to the "sacred" space, which will be just beyond them.) Parking facilities for automobiles, buses, tour-mobiles, and the handicapped will range along Ohio Drive. A granite path will lead to the entrance of the memorial, which Halprin has designed as a transition from the outside world.

Through a break in the granite wall that wends its way about the memorial and upon entering its precincts, visitors will face the Washington Monument across the Tidal Basin. Thus, connections with the heritage of the capital, the history of the country, and one of the most elemental of all commemorative forms will be established. These kinds of multiple references abound throughout the memorial. The four outdoor rooms, for example, relate to the 32nd president's four terms, the four freedoms he espoused— freedom of worship and speech, and freedom from want and fear—as well as the four primary geographical regions of the nation— North, South, East, and West. The water motifs also meld a variety of themes by alluding to Roosevelt's tenure as Secretary of the U.S. Navy, his love for his summer home at Campobello, Maine, the cures he took for polio at Warm Springs, Georgia, his role in establishing the Tennessee Valley Authority, and even Halprin's deep feelings about his own service on a destroyer in the Pacific during World War II.

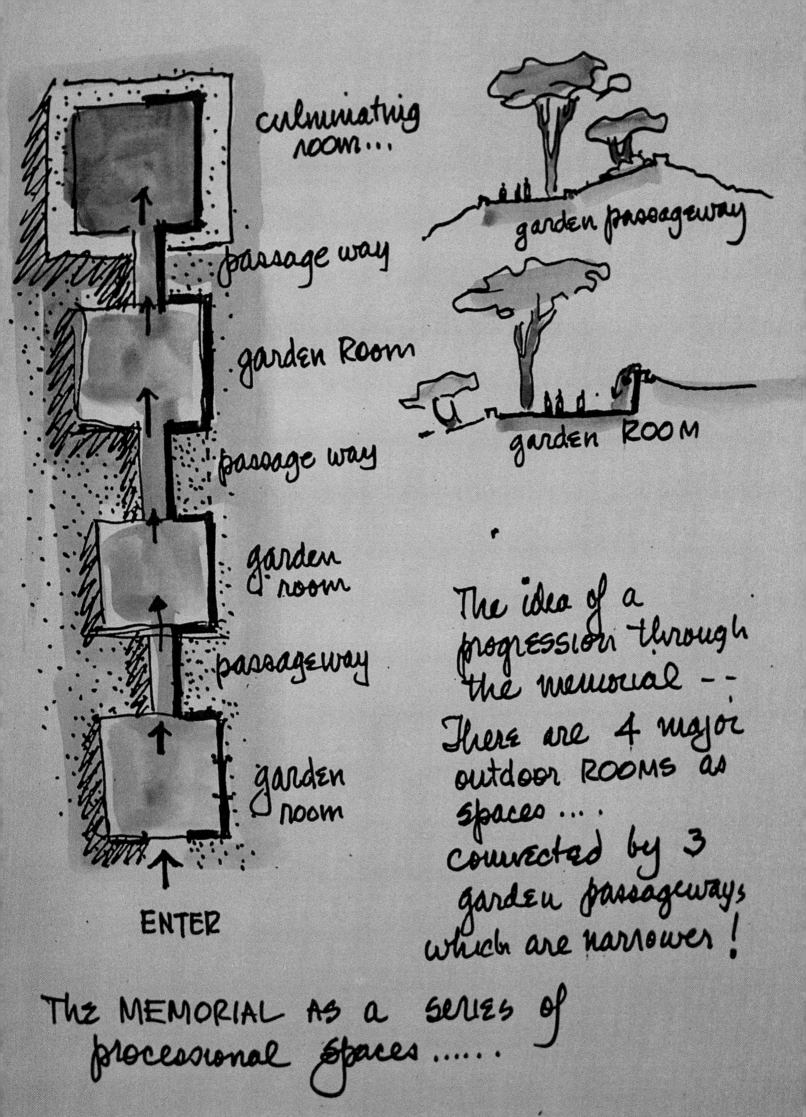

culminating room...

passage way

garden Room

passage way

garden room

passageway

garden room

ENTER

garden passageway

garden ROOM

The idea of a progression through the memorial --
There are 4 major outdoor ROOMS as spaces ...
connected by 3 garden passageways which are narrower!

The MEMORIAL AS a series of processional spaces ......

Some aspects even overlap. The culminating waterfalls of the memorial fulfill many functions. They figuratively make you feel that you have arrived in some rugged region of the Western states. As abstractions, they convey sound and movement. They are practical, too. Their thunderous roar masks the noise from airplanes flying into and out of National Airport closeby.

The sculptures by Baskin, Estern, Graham, and Segal will similarly enhance the memorial in a number of ways. However, originally Halprin had planned to include only one three-dimensional image of Roosevelt, and he was uncertain whether he wanted a standing statue or one that was seated. In his notes from 12 March 1974 he indicated that he would like something "bigger than life, standing with cape and cane and braces—because that's how most of us remember [FDR]." Four days later Halprin changed his mind. At that time he also admitted to himself, "The statue issue is a tough one in terms of scale. Also should [FDR] be seated as he normally was when we saw him or standing…I think sitting is better—but how?" Six months later he still had not resolved this matter nor what guidelines to formulate for a competition to find an appropriate artist.

By March 1975, Halprin decided the memorial should be "based on principles of *multiples*—i.e.: multiple access, multiple images of FDR, multiple sculptures, multiple spaces, etc." When he was asked recently why he altered his plans, Halprin responded: "The sculpture was the one major shift I made. I'd been thinking of big things, and then I said, 'That's all wrong.'" He realized he needed a number of pieces by many sculptors. And whoever was selected could then participate more actively in the preliminary stages.

Halprin wanted representational sculpture. He has said, "What I do in an environment is like abstract sculpture and I didn't need more. I wanted to communicate a human quality of passion. I wanted to give people a way to identify." When Julio Gonzalez executed *The Montserrat*—and Pablo Picasso, his *Guernica*; Joan Miró, the *Catalan Reaper*; and Alexander Calder, the *Almaden Mercury Fountain*— for the Spanish Loyalist Pavilion at the Paris World's Fair of 1937, they all had a similar agenda for placing art before the public. At first Gonzalez made a maquette of an abstract image with a sickle. It was a successful sculpture, only it was not direct enough to convey the way war was wracking his homeland. So, Gonzalez abandoned his signature style and instead created a recognizable figure that addresses a situation anyone can understand.

Halprin also realized that the art should be cast in bronze. The sculpture would then be the same color as the granite blocks against which it would be viewed, thus bringing alive the entire wall with scenes and people from the 1930s and 1940s. At one point the wall will even be reduced to a jumble of blocks and sculptures abstractly and figuratively

Franklin Delano Roosevelt
Memorial, 1976, Washington,
D.C. Model by Leonard Baskin
of Roosevelt's profile.

Franklin Delano Roosevelt Memorial, 1976, Washington, D.C. John Benson carving Roosevelt's name in the agate granite. Benson, the country's foremost stonemason, has been commissioned to carve all Roosevelt's quotations into the wall.

Far left:
Franklin Delano Roosevelt Memorial, 1976, Washington, D.C. One of four cylindrical-shaped maquettes by Robert Graham depicting scenes from the various social programs begun by Roosevelt.

Franklin Delano Roosevelt
Memorial, 1976, Washington, D.C.
A maquette made of polyester resin
of a standing figure of Roosevelt.
By Leonard Baskin.

depicting the tumult of the war years.

Halprin had a surprising number of artists to choose from at a time when the art world was dominated by abstract sculptors. Once Baskin, Estern, Graham, and Segal were selected, the San Franciscan "scored" a workshop for his new collaborators. The architect and the four sculptors met for four days from nine in the morning until midnight. Halprin arrived with hundreds of xeroxes of photographs of FDR and his times and tacked these to a wall that was almost eighty feet long. He also brought a dolly upon which each artist could lie and be rolled along to analyze the sheet-sized images in relation to the wall.

As a group they adopted what Segal termed "a visionary proposal." According to Segal, "The memorial will contain a narrative history of the times under a brilliant president rather than an effigy of a leader. It will be a physical and mental history consisting of the most telling images." Like Egyptian pyramids and temples, the FDR Memorial will be encrusted with the records of the life of a nation. But the sculptures in West Potomac Park will be more democratic than Old Kingdom complexes because they will also celebrate common people.

Segal has already cast his *Appalachian Farm Couple, 1936.* He will also create a bread line, an assembly line, a man hunched over a radio intently listening to one of FDR's speeches, an image of the Holocaust, and two works dealing with the destructions of war. Graham will model a series of low reliefs that will be the contemporary equivalents of the WPA murals made for post offices and public schools

Franklin Delano Roosevelt Memorial, 1976, Washington, D.C. A full-size plaster model of *Appalachian Farm Couple, 1936*, by George Segal.

Franklin Delano Roosevelt Memorial, 1976, Washington, D.C. Halprin working on a storyboard depicting important images and quotations from Roosevelt's life.

during the thirties, five columns or cylinders treating comparable themes, as well as six cubes covered with groups of letters that will honor the "alphabet agencies" of Roosevelt's administration. Baskin's giant relief of FDR as commander-in-chief on the bridge of a naval vessel with his head and upper torso in profile will be installed on a wall that leads to and from the Jefferson Memorial. Another large relief by Baskin depicting the cortege at the president's funeral will be near the gateway to the memorial as well as its termination point, if you choose to walk along the cherry tree path. It will be installed to the left of the entrance on a sixty-foot-long, sixteen-foot-high wall behind which lies an interpretive center with a media room, a two-hundred-seat theater, a small museum, a bookstore, and dining areas, as well as other service and staff facilities.

Halprin has been able to coordinate so many complex elements within the memorial by "scoring" his designs. He has orchestrated the way sunlight and shade will be directed. The images of the president and his times will be displayed chronologically, but Halprin has also calibrated how they will puncture the wall and interact with the water themes. He has analyzed the roles of various sounds, including the ambient noise of people, flowing water, and arriving and departing cars.

He has identified spots for gathering and for contemplation. A score has been written for planting new trees, retaining old ones with their magnificent canopies, and adding roses, azaleas, and flowering trees. There is even a program for the meandering wall: one side will seal you in the memorial while the other is left open toward the Tidal Basin. Above all, movement through different kinds of spaces has been carefully choreographed.

Halprin has not opted for a formal, processional sequence of circulation. He feels that the axial organization of a place such as Versailles is not appropriate in this situation because Roosevelt and his career were multi-faceted. According to Halprin, the linear progressions at Versailles or in Peking that are based on bilateral symmetry are "cool, organized, systematic, and orderly." He prefers a route through the FDR Memorial that is "hot, changeable, full of energy, and ambiguities." The initial spaces are serene; the latter ones, complex. He is interested in making you stop and start, in bringing you close to the wall and drawing you back from it. Even the granite has been chosen with this in mind. The stone blocks from the Dakotas, which consist of variegated red agate granite, will range from pinks to deep reddish brown depending on where you are, what time of day it is, and what season it is.

The FDR Memorial is as much a spatial experience as a record of the thirties and

fourties. Although it is filled with objects—whether in the form of sculptures, a canopy of trees, or rivulets of water—the memorial is not object-oriented. It is, in Halprin's words, "a totality not limited to any of its parts." Halprin is aware that the memorial will change over time. Like his nineteenth-century predecessor, Frederick Law Olmsted, he has taken into account both conceptual and social uses. He has brought nature back to our cities wherever he has worked—outdoors and downtown as well as the interior of an office building like the Crocker Bank in Los Angeles. Now he has tackled a way to present history humanistically, and, in the process, has transformed lessons from the past into a vibrant present.

Halprin and his collaborators have created such a dynamic portrait of a great president and dramatic events that when Roosevelt and his administration are merely items in a textbook, visitors to Washington, D.C., will be able to retrieve their memory more fully. An anonymous writer has described how, by passing through the memorial, we will be able to appreciate the 32nd president's "complexity, intelligence, compassion, wit, energy, and devotion to a people in need, and the multiplicity of issues and challenges both Roosevelt and the people of the nation faced during that time." In the FDR Memorial, we will be able to feel, touch, hear, smell, and, in other ways, connect with a time that once was.

Franklin Delano Roosevelt Memorial, 1976, Washington, D.C. Mock-up of agate granite wall from Cold Springs, Minnesota.

Far left:
Franklin Delano Roosevelt Memorial, 1976, Washington, D.C. Model of site plan looking north toward the memorial's entrance.

For the FDR Memorial, the sculpture search, the creative workshops with the selected sculptors, the Glen Fleck film produced to present the final design, and the report to Congress were RoundHouse projects, a partnership formed in 1975 of Sue Yung Li Ikeda and Lawrence Halprin. A further reference to RoundHouse and its activities appears in The Chronology on page 141.

Re-viewing Jerusalem *by Teddy Kollek*

TEDDY KOLLEK *emigrated to Israel in 1934 and was a founder of the NBR Kibbutz in Ein-Gev in 1937. He worked in the political department for the Jewish Agency during World War II and as a liaison for the Jewish underground. Mayor of Jerusalem since 1969, Kollek is chairman of the board of the Israel National Museum, Jerusalem, and is the author of* Sacred City of Mankind *(1968) and* Pilgrims to the Holy Land *(1970).*

Far right:
Mosque of Omar (also known as Dome of the Rock). A photograph of Jerusalem taken from the Mount of Olives.

View of Jerusalem from Moshe Safdie's apartment balcony. In the foreground is the Wailing Wall and in the background, the Mosque of Omar, built by Muslims on the site of the destroyed Temple of Solomon dating back before Christ. The surviving wall of the Temple of Solomon is now the Wailing Wall. Drawing by Lawrence Halprin from his notebooks.

When Lawrence Halprin was blasting the Jerusalem Master Plan in the 1970 Jerusalem Committee, I knew we were in trouble. This was a man I had known for years as a true friend of Jerusalem and a personal friend of mine, a man often called upon to defend us and our achievements here in Jerusalem. Back in the 1960s, when Jerusalem was still a divided city, I remember driving with Larry late one night. We stopped at the area above Mamilla, then the border between our part of Jerusalem and the old walled city, which was held by the Jordanians. We started across the valley and commiserated over the fact that the city was divided. He commented on memories from his early years here when the city was one, remembering the picturesque qualities of the ancient city behind the walls, the camels and donkeys, the ancient bazaars, and that his love for the city was deep. He complained again and again about what we were doing in Jerusalem. Finally, I exploded at him: "We know things are wrong with the city, don't just complain, tell us what to do about it!"

Years later, after the city had been reunited, here was this man, by now a distinguished and experienced professional, tearing apart Jerusalem's much labored and important master plan. The Jerusalem Committee, and particularly its town-planning subcommittee, had been set up by me to be a sounding board for our planning decisions, to help me evaluate proposals, and give me informed feedback on how to plan for our city's future. Bruno Zevi and many other committee members were speaking to the same purpose, trying to save Jerusalem from the mistakes of so many other Western metropolises—mistakes which were already clear to them and which we did not need to repeat here, such as ramming an eight-lane highway next to the two-thousand-year-old city, filling our beautiful hills with high-rise buildings, and violating a centuries-old rule of building with our native stone. I remember Larry asking me, in the late hours of that long-ago night, if it would be too difficult for me to challenge the premises of this master plan; that he and the others were sensitive to my problems as mayor. I said to him, "You all

worry about the professional issues, and let me worry about my own political problems."

I listened to them, and the rest is already an important legend in the history of Jerusalem planning, and even of planning in general. We are determined to maintain our indigenous character, even though in some instances the only way we can prevent more high-rise buildings is to buy back land from developers and purchase the development rights ourselves.

Larry's influence on Jerusalem's planning goes far beyond the Jerusalem Committee of which he is one of the most dedicated, consistent, and outspoken members. His influence stems from his deep emotional involvement with Israel, which has been nurtured over many years and experiences here. Larry spent three formative years as a teenager pioneering in Kibbutz Ein Hashofeth. He studied in the Rehavia Gymnasium. Since then he has returned again and again to Jerusalem, participating in its planning and design the way one would do in one's own hometown. He has worked on the Hadassah Hospital, the Hebrew University Givat Ram campus, and the Israel National Museum. He

Above:
Hebrew University, Givat Ram Campus, 1957, Jerusalem. Entrance fountain.

Hadassah Hebrew University Medical Center, 1966, Ein Karem, Israel. Plaza and fountain adjacent to Chagall's stained-glass windows.

Ida Crown Plaza, 1966, Jerusalem.
Detail of the entrance plaza to the
Israel National Museum.

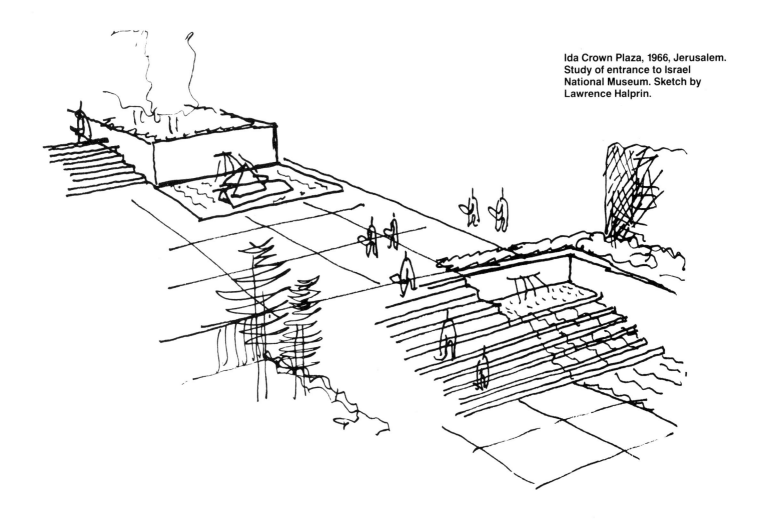

Ida Crown Plaza, 1966, Jerusalem.
Study of entrance to Israel
National Museum. Sketch by
Lawrence Halprin.

To Zion gate + parking

car tunnel into undergrd parking....

column of ayubic gate inside

To Dawg gate.

PROPOSED: New Pedestrian GATE to Eurish quarter IN Turkish tower & ON axis with the ROMAN Cardo...

Above:
The Rovah Buildings and Garden, 1980, Jerusalem. The pedestrian gate entrance into the Jewish Quarter. Drawing by Lawrence Halprin.

Ben Yehuda Street Studies, 1979, Jerusalem. The heavily congested downtown street prior to implementation of study.

Far right:
Ben Yehuda Street Studies, 1979, Jerusalem. Following implementation of study.

was involved in the initial thinking of Ben Yehuda Mall, the bus terminal in the Jewish Quarter, the ingenious solution for the car entrance under the Old City wall, and a large landscaped plaza at the end of the Cardo, which has not, as yet, been carried out. His influence lies not only in designing the entrance to the university campus, or the beautiful walk toward the museum, but goes much deeper by establishing an awareness of the architectural and environmental needs in these projects in this city.

My encounters with Larry, over the years, have helped me to formulate a planning policy for Jerusalem that looks at the large open spaces and gardens as the backbone of the city and endeavors to protect this essential structure through the legal and political means at our disposal. Two of Larry's most significant contributions have been to convince us of the importance of citizen's participation in our planning process for Jerusalem, and to teach us the techniques he has developed for making that process positive and fruitful. Whenever I see him, I complain bitterly about how all this has complicated my already complex life as mayor. Still in our kind of democracy based on our value of diversity and my perception of Jerusalem—not as a melting pot, but as a rich mosaic of people, ideas, and cultures—it is a meaningful and vital addition to our city.

Above:
Armon Hanatziv Master Plan, 1979,
Jerusalem. Model showing the
belvedere of the Haas Promenade.
Arches reflect the ancient
aqueduct originally on the site,
which brought water from the
Pools of Solomon.

Armon Hanatziv Master Plan, 1979,
Jerusalem. Model of belvedere,
a place from which to view the
Old City.

Far left:
Walter and Elise Haas Promen-
dade, 1984, Jerusalem. Maquette
of lighting study for the promenade.

Walter and Elise Haas Promenade,
1984, Jerusalem.

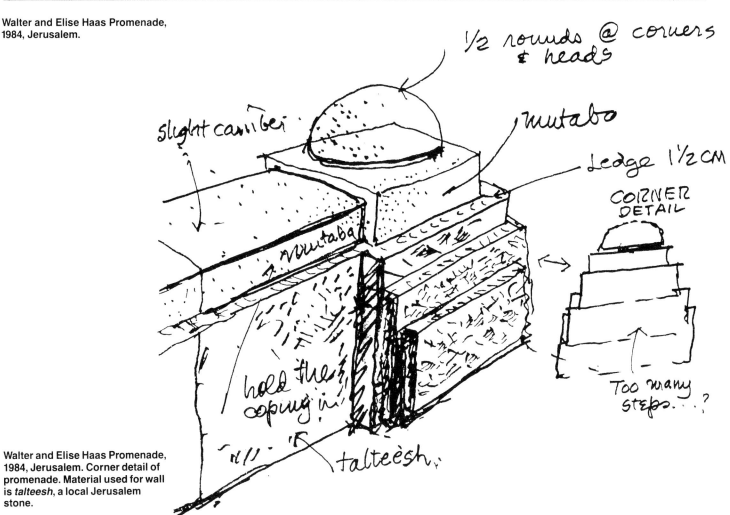

Walter and Elise Haas Promenade,
1984, Jerusalem. Corner detail of
promenade. Material used for wall
is *talteesh*, a local Jerusalem
stone.

½ rounds @ corners
& heads

mutaba

slight camber

mutaba

mutaba

Ledge 1½ CM

CORNER
DETAIL

hold the
coping in

Too many
steps....?

talteesh

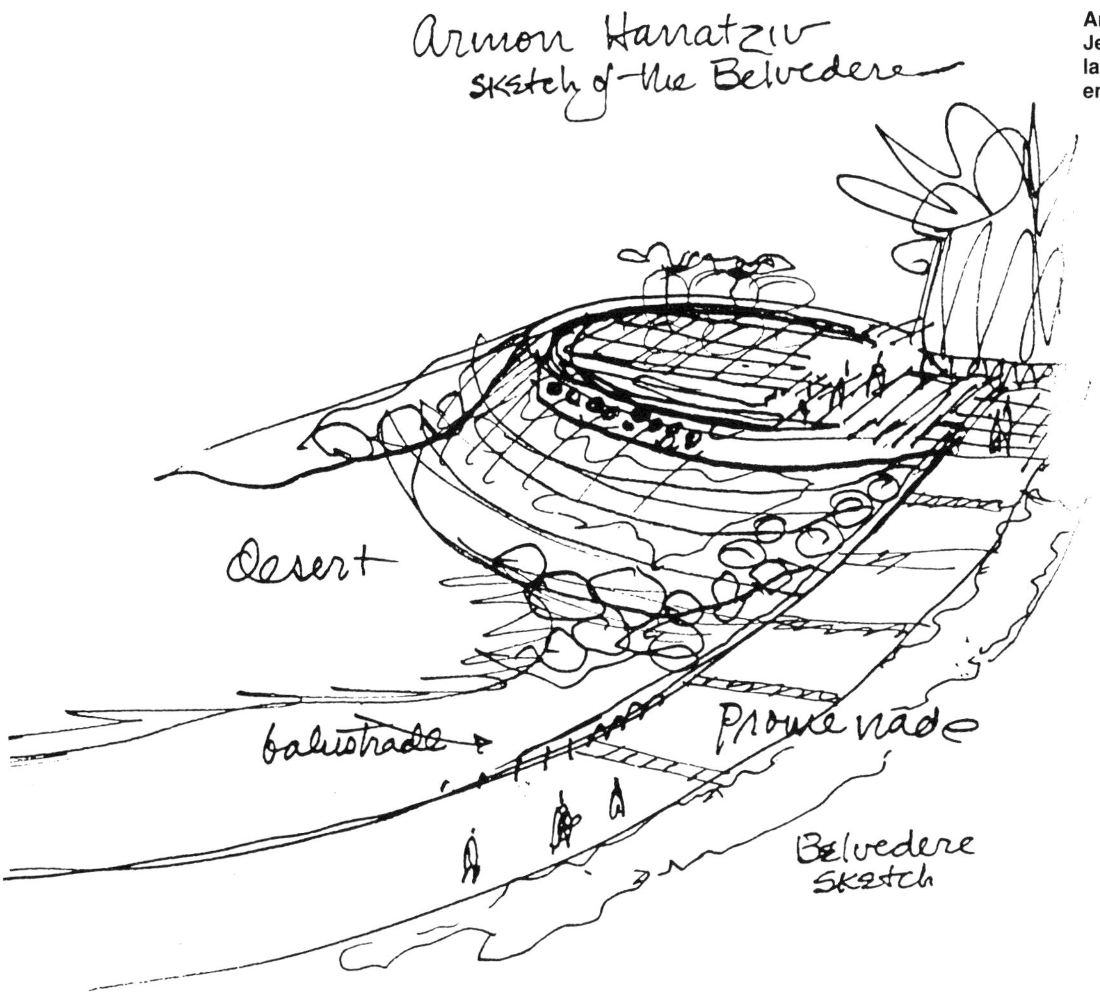

Armon Hanatziv
sketch of the Belvedere

Desert

balustrade →

Promenade

Belvedere
Sketch

Armon Hanatziv Master Plan, 1979, Jerusalem. Sketch showing the relationship between Haas Promenade and belvedere.

At the present time, Larry is still involved in building Jerusalem, as he has been in the recent past. Right now his Walter and Elise Haas Promenade is under construction. This promenade, next to the United Nations Headquarters, overlooks the whole of Jerusalem. When finished, it will be the most important addition to the landscape of Jerusalem in the past twenty years.

Many distinguished architects and planners have added their genius to the blessing of Jerusalem. However, I can't think of many in recent times whose involvement and influence in theory and practice has been as long lasting and important as that of Lawrence Halprin. And I think (and I suspect Larry thinks so, too) that, deeply, he is a Jerusalemite first.

The Chronology

Samuel and Rose Halprin.

Halprin with his mother, Rose.

Cornell University baseball team.

1916

1 July. Birth of Lawrence Halprin to Samuel W. Halprin and Rose Luria Halprin, their first child in Brooklyn, New York. Samuel is president of *Landseas* scientific instruments export firm. Rose is national president of Hadassah, the women's Zionist organization, and chairperson of the American branch of the Jewish Agency for Palestine.

1920s

Halprin begins to draw and paint.

1924

Birth of Halprin's sister, Ruth.

1929–1933

Attends Brooklyn Polytechnic Preparatory Country Day School for Boys. Plays football, tennis, basketball, and baseball. Halprin is awarded "High School Pitcher of the Year" in 1932 and 1933.

1933–1935

Halprin makes his first trip to Palestine and helps with the founding of Kibbutz En Hashofeth, near Haifa. During this time, he works in a factory extracting potash and other chemicals from the Dead Sea, and labors as a ranch hand by day and by night guards the kibbutz on horseback.

1935–1939

Attends Cornell University School of Agriculture, Ithaca, New York. Summers are spent working on farms in the Midwest and New England. Halprin plays baseball on the university team and hopes for a pitching career in professional baseball. Receives B.S. in plant sciences.

1939–1941

Attends University of Wisconsin, Madison, Department of Horticulture, while working as a research and teaching assistant. Thesis is

Larry and Anna Halprin soon after they were married.

Anna Halprin with Walter Gropius at a costume ball.

A costumed Anna and Larry.

on photoperiod (the optimum length of daylight hours needed for normal plant growth) and its effect on flowering plants. Receives M.S. in horticulture.

Becomes a weekend painter.

1940

September. Marries fellow student/dancer Anna Schuman.

Visits Frank Lloyd Wright's Taliesin Community in Spring Green, Wisconsin. Soon after, Halprin reads Christopher Tunnard's book, *Gardens in the Modern Landscape* (Architectural Press, London, 1938) and becomes aware of the significance of design in the environment. Decides on the spot to study design in architecture, with emphasis on landscape design.

1942–1944

Receives scholarship to Harvard University Graduate School of Design, Cambridge, Massachusetts. Studies under architecture professors Walter Gropius, Marcel Breuer, and landscape architect Christopher Tunnard, whose book had so influenced Halprin. While at Harvard, Halprin meets and becomes close friends with San Francisco architect William Wurster and his wife, Cathrine Bauer Wurster, an important social planner. Is also vitally influenced by lecturer László Moholy Nagy. Classmates include Philip Johnson, I.M. Pei, Edward Larrabee Barnes, and Paul Rudolph.

Leaves Harvard in December 1943 to enlist in the U.S. Navy (receives B.L.A. in January 1944). Serves as lieutenant junior grade on the destroyer USS *Morris* on tour throughout the Pacific. While on offshore picket duty during the invasion of Okinawa, Halprin's ship is cut in half by a kamikaze plane, sending him to San Francisco on survivor's leave. Serves in the navy through April 1945.

One of the many sketches Halprin makes while in the navy. Christmas Eve on Amsterdam Island.

Thomas D. Church.

"A typical yard" published in *House Beautiful*.

Contoured lines of the Donnell Garden.

Organic paving pattern of the Schuman Garden.

1945

Begins employment in the San Francisco office of landscape architect Thomas D. Church.

Purchases a small tract house in Mill Valley, California, which had been constructed to house workers from the nearby shipyards of Sausalito. Halprin remodels the house and creates a small backyard garden that is later published in *Sunset* magazine and becomes Halprin's first demonstration of how design can enhance people's lives—in this case for families after the war.

1947

Promoted to an associate in Church's firm.

Writes an article with Thomas Church on "Backyard Gardens" for the magazine *House Beautiful*.

Begins a series of ongoing collaborations with his wife, Anna Halprin, who, in the 1960s will become a major force in the dance world for her staging of avant-garde performances. Halprin designs costumes and stage sets for these performances.

1948

Co-publishes *Impulse* dance magazine with Anna Halprin.

December. First daughter, Daria, is born.

Donnell Garden, Sonoma County, California. While still employed by Church, Halprin designs one of his first gardens to relate to the land's natural contours. He curves the defining edges of the swimming pool to follow the lines of the surrounding land and hills. Sculpture by Adaline Kent, an important Bay Area sculptor, is used as the focal point of the pool.

1949

First visits Phoenix Lake in Marin County, a place where he will spend many hours hiking, sketching, and observing nature through its varying moods and seasonal changes over the next thirty-five years.

September. Opens own landscape architecture firm—Lawrence Halprin—in San Francisco.

Schuman Garden, Woodside, California. Halprin designs his first major garden in collaboration with architect William Wurster for his in-laws, Mr. and Mrs. I. Schuman. On a four-acre site, the house and garden cover one acre, while the remaining acreage is maintained in its natural state as a meadow. Halprin begins to express his concern for the relationship and integration between elements—here, the integration between the natural terrain with the man-made garden. Completed 1950.

1950

October. Presents lecture, "Landscape Architecture in a Changing World," at the Institute for Modern Living, University of Washington, Seattle. This is the first major conference on modern design following the Second World War and is shared with two other guest speakers, Richard Neutra and Charles Eames.

First visits Big Sur on the northern California coast. Becomes fascinated with the rugged, mountainous landscape and its interface with the ocean, along with the area's avant-garde, alternative lifestyles. Halprin and his family return often to visit painter Louisa Jenkins, anthropologist Maude Oakes, and sculptor David Tollerton.

Caygill Garden, Orinda, California. This project, a residential garden located on a hillside ridge, represents the first design in which Halprin uses running water in his landscapes—in this case, a wading pool with fountain utilizing river-washed stones from Big Sur instead of plantings. Completed 1951.

Esherick Garden, Kentfield, California. Through the design of this residential garden, Halprin is introduced to architect Joseph Esherick, and they begin the first of many collaborations exploring the integration of houses and gardens as works of environmental design. Completed 1952.

Marin General Hospital, Novato, California. Halprin's first commission to design a public garden space. His involvement in solving design problems is beginning to address larger and more complex issues: from small private gardens answering the needs of an individual family, to larger public spaces having to meet the needs of many. In this plan he incorporates roads, walkways, gardens, sculpture, and activity areas appropriate for ambulatory patients. Completed 1952.

Woerner Garden, Kentfield, California. The blending of the cultivated landscape with the natural hillside is the significant design feature of this narrow garden on the flanks of Mount Tamalpais. The man-made garden of gray and textured plants is interwoven with the surrounding native chaparrel. With architect John Fink. Completed 1952.

1951

Simon Roof Garden, San Francisco. Working within a four-foot-square grid system, Halprin establishes a relationship between the formal, modular framework of a traditional garden design and a seemingly random disposition of plants and rocks. Gravel and redwood decking become the unifying features, while plant containers, stones from Big Sur, bamboos, succulents, and tufted grasses provide variety and highlights. The result raises the idea of a tar and gravel roof to new levels. Completed 1952; first of Halprin's gardens to be published internationally.

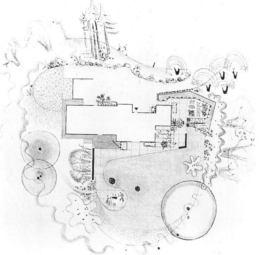

Patio designed as a natural form for the Caygill Garden.

Big Sur, south of San Francisco on the California coast.

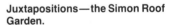

Site plan for Joseph Esherick's residence.

Juxtapositions—the Simon Roof Garden.

The young Halprin family, Anna and Larry with Daria and Rana.

Dance Deck.

Greenhouse of Red Hill Nursery.

1952

June. Second daughter, Rana, is born.

Master Plan and Report for University of California, Davis. Working with campus-architect Robert Evans, Halprin devises his first master plan that includes both the design of the landscape and the placement of the buildings into a complex community. The plan represents the conversion of a small 3,000-student agricultural college to a 27,000-student, multidisciplined university. Halprin is beginning to see his work not only as landscape design but more as environmental design, whereby he must consider the environment in its totality before building anything.

Halprin House and Garden, Kentfield, California. The Halprin family moves into a house situated on a four-acre wooded site on the eastern flank of Mount Tamalpais and designed as a series of pavilions by architect William Wurster. The garden is conceived by Halprin not as a traditional garden, but as a choreographed sequence of penetrations leading from the house, through the woods, down flights of steps to the *Dance Deck* below. Working with lighting designer Arch Lauterer, Halprin designs an outdoor redwood dance deck for his wife, Anna, who will develop many of her avant-garde approaches to theater and dance here. The deck evolves into a multifaceted place for events to happen, or as a quiet place of contemplation. Many early experiments for his future workshops are developed on the deck. Completed 1954.

United Mine Worker's Hospitals, Hazard, Harlan, Middlesboro, and Wise, Kentucky; and Whiteburg, West Virginia. Halprin is commissioned to design the grounds for five hospitals in rural hill communities of Appalachia, sponsored by the United Mine Worker's Union and a federal government planning grant. His landscape solution is a stark departure from traditional hospital grounds, in that the hospitals are treated as community centers surrounded by gardens that include spaces for performing and social activities. Moreland Smith, architect. Completed 1957; receives P/A Design Award, Health, 1954.

Red Hill Nursery, San Anselmo, California. One of only a few buildings Halprin himself designs. The site slopes steeply down to a creek, and includes a retail plant nursery and a landscape contracting business. To increase the site's usability, Halprin extends a deck out over the creek. The modular-frame building is made of glass, stucco, and plywood panels with an overall intent to blend indoor and outdoor elements. Completed 1953.

1953

November. Nominated by *Time* magazine and the San Francisco Chamber of Commerce as "One of San Francisco's Leaders of Tomorrow."

Bissinger Garden, Kentfield, California. This plan represents an early example of satellite houses broken up to incorporate the gardens. The site is hilly, with gardens, pool, and terraces separating various parts of the house. William Wurster, architect. Completed 1955; receives AIA Award of Merit, 1957.

Easter Hill Village, Richmond, California. In an old abandoned rock quarry, Halprin and architect Vernon DeMars establish an individually designed approach for a low-income housing development through designed streetscapes and the use of a multicolored palette. Rather than remove the left-over boulders, some of which are enormous, each rock is numbered to be later moved by bulldozers and set in place by the contractor. Completed 1955; receives *House and Home,* Special Award for Land Planning, 1956.

Kaufman Garden, San Rafael, California. Working with a steep site, Halprin integrates the garden and swimming pool into the natural contours of the hillside. The pool is treated as an artistic element with a Ray Rice sculpture spewing water into the pool, providing sound and motion. Completed 1954.

Greenwood Common, Berkeley, California. On a 2½-acre site purchased and subdivided by William Wurster into twelve individual lots and a shared open space, Halprin designs five of the private gardens and a common area as a centerpiece for the development. Addressing the idea that suburbs lack communal parks, each lot has access to the half-acre common, while each house sits on a small, private, low-maintenance lot skirting the common. The plan allows all residents to enjoy a view of San Francisco and the Golden Gate Bridge. This project will later influence Halprin's approach to The Sea Ranch by clustering houses around a shared common space. Gardens include *Ackerman Garden, Baer Garden, Maenchen Garden, Schaff Garden,* and *Wurster Garden.* Completed 1958.

Landscape Master Plan for University of California, Berkeley. This large-scale master plan represents an early concept of maintaining open space amidst a huge building program, and is one of the first projects to use street furniture as part of its comprehensive plan. Later, with architects Vernon DeMars and Donald Reay, Halprin designs the grounds for the *Student Union* and *Sproul Plaza,* the monumental entranceway into the university. Additional designs are commissioned for the *Alumni House,* with architect Clarence Mayhew, and for the renovation of the 1903 outdoor *Greek Theatre,* with architect Ernest Born, for whom Halprin acted as consultant. Completed 1960.

Abstract pattern of Bissinger Garden.

Easter Hill Village.

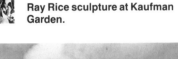

Ray Rice sculpture at Kaufman Garden.

The multifaceted Sproul Plaza, University of California, Berkeley.

Sketch of Golden Gate Baptist Theological Seminary.

Old Orchard Shopping Center.

Winter lake at Washington Water Power Corporate Headquarters.

The High Sierra—a place for inspiration and study.

1955

Weizmann Institute of Science, Rehovoth, Israel. Invited by Meyer Weisgal, director of the Weizmann Institute (named after Israel's first president Chaim Weizmann), to establish basic design principles for the continued development of this important scientific research institute. This marks Halprin's first trip to Jerusalem after the formation of the state of Israel. Surrounding the institute, he designs a greenbelt area that includes terraces, parks, and groves.

Golden Gate Baptist Theological Seminary Garden, Mill Valley, California. In collaboration with John Carl Warnecke and Lawrence Livingston, this project is Halprin's first opportunity to plan and carry out a large reforestation plan of Monterey pines intermingled with native oaks. The scheme provides the basic theme for the new campus, located on a series of rolling hills at Strawberry Point in Marin County. Completed 1958.

Old Orchard Shopping Center, Skokie, Illinois. With his first shopping center commission, Halprin further expands his studies of human interaction in relation to their environment. Instead of developing another typical corridor of shops with a parking lot in front, he designs a series of malls turning the stores inward away from the parking area and treats the complex as a community unto itself, rather than an extension of the parking lot. Halprin devises a total retail environment including gardens, graphics, and street furniture that becomes a prototype for new shopping centers where environments are created for people's enjoyment, as well as places to shop. Loebl, Schlossman & Bennett, architects. Completed 1957.

Washington Water Power Corporate Headquarters, Spokane, Washington. In an attempt to humanize the working/office environment, the buildings are grouped together to form a campus-like environment with cafeterias, picnic areas, and a lake. Represents one of the first instances where an industrial/office complex is designed with the intent to create a pleasing and stimulating locale for the workers. Brooks & Walker, architects. Completed 1959.

1956

Begins spending summers hiking, sketching, and studying in the mountains of the High Sierra. These experiences have a profound impact on Halprin's understanding and interpretation of the ecological processes and how form arises in nature.

First meets and befriends Dr. Joseph L. Henderson, who, through his interest in art, architecture, and the study of Jungian archetypes, influences Halprin both personally and professionally throughout his life.

Grant Garden.

Washington Square, the heart of North Beach.

Grant Garden, Hillsborough, California. Working closely with architect Joseph Esherick, they site the house on a hillside as the best vantage point for viewing an oak-shaded meadow. The house is linked to the garden through a series of long, wooden trellises and stone walls stepping down into the pool area. Although shapes are informal, the linkage system harks back to Italian hill town gardens. Completed 1965.

Washington Square Park Master Plan, San Francisco. Initially invited by the Telegraph Hill Neighborhood Association to redesign this popular one-acre urban park in the heart of North Beach, Halprin adds walking paths, an open lawn area, tree clusters, and a children's playground. Final drawings are carried out by Douglas Baylis.

1957

October. Becomes a member of The American Society of Landscape Architects.

Hebrew University, Givat Ram Campus, Jerusalem. Halprin devises an open-space study for the campus site located on a barren, rocky ridge. The plan calls for a series of plazas on a heavily tiered hillside and the replanting of trees indigenous to the area. This main campus of Hebrew University later becomes part of the Cultural Mile, where buildings such as Parliament, the Israel National Museum, the Shrine of the Book, and the proposed Israel Supreme Court Building—each occupying their own ridge—are linked along a several-mile-long stretch of roadway. Completed 1960.

Redwood Building, Stanford University, Stanford, California. A significant project for Halprin in that it allows him to further explore the notion of the California garden as a dry landscape. Working with indigenous plant material, his design incorporates patterned paving, running water, pleasantly scented plants, and a mosaic by Ray Rice. The project, a courtyard in a building designed by Hervey Clark, is a precursor to Halprin's internationally acclaimed McIntyre Garden. Completed 1958.

Hebrew University, Givat Ram campus.

Courtyard of the Redwood Building.

The fully integrated design of Capitol Towers Housing.

Seattle World's Fairground, Seattle. Halprin is invited to serve on a design commission with Minoru Yamasaki, Paul Thiry, Perry Johansen, and others to advise on site selection and overall development of the 1962 World's Fair. Basic to the plan is Halprin's aim to provide both an environment and buildings that can be converted to other uses after the fair's closing. He also sets forth the design for the gardens of the U.S. Science Center for which Yamasaki is the architect and Charles Eames the exhibit designer. Completed 1961.

Stanford Medical Plaza, Palo Alto, California. A unique commission in which a group of forty doctors ask William Wurster to design a medical complex and Halprin the gardens. In the plan are forty individually designed gardens adjacent to each doctor's office, plus a community garden for patient's use. Completed 1958.

Married Student's Housing, University of California, San Francisco. Planned within a grove of eucalyptus trees on a hill overlooking San Francisco, the design includes, besides housing, play areas for children, gardens, and pathways connecting to the campus. Working with architects Clark & Beuttler, and George Rockrise, Halprin integrates this medical school/hospital facility within a growing urban neighborhood. Completed 1961; receives AIA First Honor Award, 1961.

1958

Capitol Towers Housing, Sacramento, California. This landscape design and site plan are early examples of urban redevelopment. A mix of townhouses and apartment buildings around central courtyards containing swimming pools, sculpture, and fountains are designed with architects Edward Larrabee Barnes and William Wurster. Additional elements are the wall sculpture by Jacques Overhof, and street furniture and graphics by Saul Bass. Completed 1965; receives P/A First Design Award, 1959.

1959

Navajo Nation Master Development Program, Window Rock, Arizona. This master plan for the Navajo Nation headquarters and tourist center provides Halprin with his first introduction to the Southwest and to Native American settlements. Included in the plan is a survey by Halprin of the overall tree and plant population for the tri-state area of nine million acres. With architects John Carl Warnecke & Associates, and planners Livingston & Blayney. Completed 1960.

McIntyre Garden, Hillsborough, California. A residential garden drawn from early Mediterranean examples, this design represents a significant step in Halprin's search for a prototypical California garden. By utilizing hard geometric forms and surfaces, by planting in a way that creates an architectonic division of spaces, and by total exclusion of the natural environment, Halprin takes the natural and abstracts it. It is in this project that he develops his concept of capturing the essence of nature without copying it. Sounds, smells, and textures are drawn from nature, but not colors or shapes. This idea is used later in his designs for waterfalls, parks, and plazas. Further utilized and developed is the concept of movement—of moving people by inducing their participation throughout the space. This project has a major influence on garden design through its wide national and international publication. Completed 1961.

Oakbrook Shopping Center, Oakbrook, Illinois. An early shopping center design where Halprin pays special attention to graphics, lighting, integrating the parking area with the shopping center, and choreographing people's movement through the center. Shoppers are treated to the idea of "gardens for shopping," pools, and flowers in an environment that affords protection from the winds, but takes advantage of the sun's warming effects. Loebl, Schlossman & Bennett, architects. Completed 1962; receives AIA Chicago Chapter, Honor Award, 1963.

Halprin begins an ongoing series of notebooks that he uses both personally and professionally. They record his impressions, perceptions, ideas, designs, travel notes, sketches, processes, project proposals, and lists of things to do. By 1986, the categorized and indexed notebooks will number eighty-six . . .

1960

January. The firm Lawrence Halprin is incorporated into Lawrence Halprin & Associates, an interdisciplinary group of planners, landscape architects, architects, ecologists, designers, and photographers devoted to evolving experimental work that addresses broad issues of environmental design as well as social and political issues in regions, cities, and public spaces. To Halprin, the firm itself is an example of the process of collective creativity, by exemplifying in its best moments the idea that groups can work synergistically and develop into more than just the sum of its individual components: "We were full of high energy, of boundless enthusiasm, high spirits, and in an eager search for new ways of doing things!"

Lawrence Halprin & Associates, 1960.

123

Landscape as art, the Gould Garden.

Gould Garden, Berkeley, California. In this design, Halprin strives for a hard, geometric quality as a technique for sculpting the site. One descends from the house to the deck, terrace, landing, and finally to the pool and pavilion. A sculptured fountain pours water into the pool, adding sound and motion amidst a quiet planting of existing eucalyptus, Monterey pine, and live oak. Completed 1966.

Lehman Garden, Kentfield, California. Both house and garden are backed up against a large rock outcropping over which a small man-made waterfall descends into a swimming pool that appears to be carved from the rock. A mosaic by Ray Rice lies on the pool's bottom, while a deck extends above grade to connect the house with the garden. Joseph Esherick, architect. Completed 1961.

St. Francis Square, San Francisco. Sponsored by the International Longshoreman's Union and the San Francisco Redevelopment Agency, Halprin designs a master plan and landscape design for a racially integrated housing development. The key feature here is that the 300 apartments are arranged facing inward onto communal gardens and play areas, rather than outward toward the street and the automobile—as has been typical of American housing design. The plan's intent is to keep the buildings simple and to elaborate on the gardens, which are for both public and private use. Continued tenant and neighborhood participation in the garden spaces has made this housing development remarkably successful. Marquis & Stoller, architects. Completed 1963; receives FHA Honor Award, Residential, 1963 and Governor's Design Award of Exceptional Distinction, State of California, Social Improvements, 1966.

1961

Summer. Travels throughout Europe with twelve-year-old daughter Daria to study cities and towns, especially their streets, plazas, and waterfronts.

A successful investigation into urban living, St. Francis Square.

One of many sketch studies made during a lifetime of travel.

IBM Advanced Systems Development Center, Los Gatos, California. A further expression of Halprin's belief that the office environment can and should be humanized. Set within eighty acres of rolling hills, he designs a series of courtyards and gardens ranging from small controlled interior courtyards, to free-form naturalistic grounds that blend with the existing landscape. According to Halprin, "These are the architectural elements of the landscape. All are surrounded by a series of transitional plantings—from plantings quite domesticated and small in scale, to the broader scale, where the planting begins to merge, first through planted lawns, and then uncared-for plantings, to the hillside beyond." Each office opens with a view to an individually designed garden; larger gardens are incorporated to accommodate meeting and dining facilities. Hellmuth, Obata & Kassabaum, architects. Completed 1964.

Miliani New Town Development, Oahu, Hawaii. Designs a master plan for a 7,000-acre new town with a projected population of 65,000. "The essential problem in establishing a new community," says Halprin, "has been to find a kind of basic order to guide its growth, within which succeeding years and people can develop wide variegation and the sense of nonregimentation and unpredictability which creative life demands." DeMars & Reay, architects; Livingston & Blayney, planners. Completed 1968.

1962

April–May. Included in a group exhibition at San Francisco Museum of Art (later the San Francisco Museum of Modern Art), *81st Annual Painting Exhibition, San Francisco Art Institute.* Since the early 1900s, the Annual has been an important opportunity for Bay Area artists to exhibit their work.

June–July. *Works of Lawrence Halprin,* a one-person exhibition at San Francisco Museum of Art.

The Sea Ranch Master Plan, Sonoma County, California. On a 5,000-acre site, with ten miles of ocean frontage on California's northern coastline, The Sea Ranch represents a breakthrough in basing a community's development on ecological principles and calling for as little intrusion as possible into the native environment. Originally designated as a second-home, vacation community, the program calls for condominium sites, single-family residences, a restaurant, airport, golf course, village center, hotel, and recreation facilities. Halprin spends weekends camping at the site's beaches, studying effects of the weather, and mapping wind patterns for the best placement of housing. He notes, for example, that "one day out of three is either windy, foggy, or rainy. The other two are lovely."

A humanistic working environment for IBM employees at their Advanced Systems Development Center.

Looking south down The Sea Ranch coast at a condominium cluster.

Passageway at The Sea Ranch.

The greatest challenge facing Halprin is how to preserve the character of the land, while putting a relatively dense development on it. By his plan, housing is tucked into the natural framework of the hills, rather than hugging the shoreline as has been typical of California oceanfront developments. Recreational facilities, such as tennis courts and swimming pool, are sunk into the landscape to ameliorate winds and assure their invisibility on the horizon. Condominium units and individual houses are clustered to offer views and privacy while preserving maximum open space as common areas for the entire community. Wood siding and slanted roofs relate to the farms and the simple, rustic structures that were previously on the site.

The Sea Ranch is by no means virgin land—until a few years ago it was an active sheep ranch, and before that there was a long history of extensive logging and agriculture. Halprin's overall approach to The Sea Ranch establishes a system of land planning that implies a long-range involvement with the property rather than the more traditional, limited role of the designer. Charles Moore, Donlyn Lyndon, William Turnbull and Richard Whitaker (MLTW), and Joseph Esherick, architects. Completed 1967. Receives P/A Design Award, Recreation, for Sea Ranch Swim and Tennis Club, 1966; Governor's Design Award of Exceptional Distinction, State of California, Planned Communities, 1966; and AIA Award of Honor for Sea Ranch Swim and Tennis Club, 1968.

Ghirardelli Square, San Francisco. Conversion of this nineteenth-century chocolate factory begins when developer William Matson Roth purchased the site in the early sixties. Roth is inclined toward preserving and recycling the old brick structures and approaches Halprin and architects Wurster, Bernardi & Emmons for development ideas. The plan becomes a series of terraced plazas, incorporating shops, restaurants, fountains, and courtyards layered above a multilevel, underground parking garage, functioning together as a shopping center. Integrated into the plan is Halprin's desire to choreograph people's movement through ramped and winding staircases, tiered platforms and fountains, and balconies that offer views of the Bay, Alcatraz Island, and Aquatic Park. It is one of his finest examples of creating space as theater. Completed 1968. Receives AIA Award of Merit, 1966; and Governor's Design Award of Exceptional Distinction, State of California, Rehabilitation, 1966.

Ghirardelli Square.

Ghirardelli Square, viewed from the San Francisco Bay.

The much-used Embarcadero Plaza at the foot of Market Street.

San Francisco City Dance in the Embarcadero Plaza.

Embarcadero Plaza and Fountain (now M. Justin Herman Plaza), San Francisco. Situated at the foot of Market Street, the city's main east-west thoroughfare, and adjacent to the Ferry Building, the waterfront, and an elevated freeway, this four-acre plaza is conceived by Halprin as a gathering place for outdoor events and festivals. Focal point of the plaza is a fountain designed in collaboration with Armand Vaillancourt. The monumental, concrete structure is designed to echo the force of the nearby freeway and to encourage people's movement through, under, and in it. Halprin's adjoining *Ferry Park* demonstrates the integration of elevated freeways and green parks running underneath as beautiful and usable urban parkland. With Mario Ciampi & Associates, and John Bolles & Associates, architects. Completed 1972; receives HUD Design Award, 1974.

Nicollet Avenue Mall, Minneapolis, Minnesota. Halprin pioneers one of the first conversions of a downtown street into a pedestrian and transit mall. Designed to keep downtown businesses and their customers from fleeing to the suburbs, his plan calls for the closing of an eight-block section of Nicollet Avenue to all traffic except buses, service vehicles, and pedestrians. To encourage pedestrian movement, the wide and curving streetscape is designed to offer places to sit, with graphics, sculpture, fountains, and various plantings of trees and flowers along the way. Since the mall's opening, major new buildings and second-

level pedestrian crossings have since been constructed in the area, assuring the continued vitality of downtown Minneapolis. Completed 1967.

Northpark Shopping Center, Dallas. An early example of an eighty-acre, regional shopping center designed by Halprin and built around an enclosed interior space. Commissioned by Raymond Nasher, designed by Kevin Roche for Eero Saarinen & Associates, and Harrell & Hamilton, architects. Completed 1965.

What To Do About Market Street? Realizing that Market Street is to be torn up for the underground construction of the Bay Area Rapid Transit System (BART), the San Francisco Planning and Research Agency (SPUR), a newly formed citizen's group for good planning, commissions Halprin and others to prepare a prospectus for future development along Market Street. With Livingston & Blayney, planners; Rockrise & Watson, architects.

San Francisco Freeways Report. In a further departure from the confines of traditional landscape architecture, Halprin begins to concern himself with the urban influence of transportation and its impact on cities. In this study, to be submitted to the California Department of Highways and required by the San Francisco Board of Supervisors *before* proceeding with freeway design in San Francisco, Halprin examines the nature of freeways in cities and develops a series of new design criteria in which freeways and buildings can be integrated. Completed 1964.

Nighttime drama, the Seattle
Center Fountain.

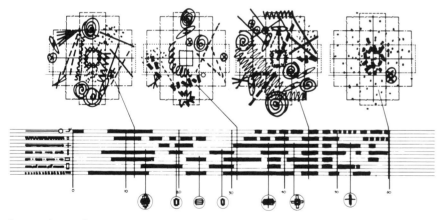

A score, for the Seattle Center
Fountain.

Seattle Center, Seattle. Halprin converts the
seventy-five-acre site of the 1962 World's
Fair—of which he served on the original
design commission—into a permanent park
and cultural center with museums, theaters,
amusements, restaurants, fountains, and
picnic areas. Paul Thiry, architect.
Completed 1964.

1963

Panhandle Freeway Plan and Report.
Appointed by the California Department
of Highways—a bold step in itself since
freeway design typically is left in the hands
of engineers—Halprin proposes his
controversial plans for a "Panhandle Parkway
and Crosstown Tunnel" in San Francisco.
Offering four alternate plans, his main
contention is that the freeway not go
through Golden Gate Park, but go *under*
the park in tunnels. Other recommendations
brought out in the report include the
following: that a curvilinear freeway not
be built within the city, since it cuts
through the existing grid; that an urban
freeway go between, not through,
neighborhoods; and that multilevel freeways
work best in urban situations and must be
integrated with and built as part of a total
community development. Widespread media
opposition to the plan (incorrectly implying
that the freeway will cut through the park)
leads to the plan's outright rejection.

Woodlake Apartments, San Mateo, California.
This thirty-acre, 994-unit housing complex
is designed as a self-sufficient suburban
community. Like Halprin's early shopping
center designs, where he turned the shops
inward away from the street environment,
here the plan is also turned inward, centering
on a large open-space area for community
use. All structures are kept at the periphery
of the site and located over parking, so that
the center open space is kept free from both
buildings and vehicles, allowing for tenant's
uninterrupted use. Also included in the plan
are a complete shopping center, recreational
facilities, and private landscaped courtyards.
This is his first opportunity to work with
Gerson Bakar, a developer with whom
Halprin collaborates on several later
projects. The project becomes a model of
high-density suburban design. Wurster,
Bernardi & Emmons, architects.
Completed 1966.

Turning the street inward at the
Woodlake Apartments.

Gardens for University of California, Santa Cruz. Halprin further refines his cluster-style designs in this landscape plan for three interrelated college campuses located in the redwoods of the Santa Cruz mountains. In an effort to preserve the natural vegetation, the architects design village clusters, each with their own sense of identity and community where students live and study. Each cluster includes landscaped courtyards off which are housing and dining facilities. Completed 1967. Stevenson College, with architect Joseph Esherick, receives AIA Honor Award, 1968; Crown College, with architect Ernest Kump, receives Fourth Biennial HUD Award, 1970; Cowell College, with architects Wurster, Bernardi & Emmons, receives P/A Design Award, Education, 1964.

University of California, Santa Cruz.

1964

July. Awarded The American Institute of Architects Medal for Allied Professions.

Begins studies on systems of scoring and visual notations of motion, coined "motations," to record and communicate movement through the environment. This scoring process is similar to labanotation, a dancer's way of recording choreographed movement. Scores and scoring are major developments for Halprin, who uses them to energize creativity in many fields. (See *The RSVP Cycles* for a complete description.)

Halprin Cabin, The Sea Ranch, California. As a result of Halprin's early involvement at The Sea Ranch, he acquires a five-acre site on a peninsula overlooking the ocean that contains Indian mounds and native rock formations. With driftwood from the beach, he constructs a small amphitheater where some of his later workshops are conducted. The house becomes an early prototype of houses built at The Sea Ranch, exemplifying many of the design principles designated in the original plan. With architects Charles Moore and William Turnbull.

The amphitheater for play and performance at the Halprin cabin.

Appointed Urban Design Consultant to San Francisco's Bay Area Rapid Transit District (BART). Halprin establishes design and planning criteria that results in the report, *Bay Area Rapid Transit Urban Design and Open Space Criteria Master Plan.* He uses scoring as a new approach to describe the protection and enhancement of environmental amenities *before* a transit system is built. Due to major philosophical and planning differences, Halprin resigns in 1966 when the BART board refuses to combine its construction with the criteria he had recommended to soften the transit system's impact on the community. With Donn Emmons, architect. Plan not implemented.

Bank of America Headquarters, San Francisco. With architects Wurster, Bernardi & Emmons, and Pietro Belluschi, Halprin acts as design consultant and landscape architect on this fifty-five-story downtown office building and plaza. Following a trip to Devils

Bank of America Headquarters.

Custom House Plaza atop a traffic tunnel.

Custom House Plaza atop a traffic tunnel.

Inner courtyard of Northpoint Apartments.

A visit to Tivoli Gardens, part of the Dancers' Workshop trip to Scandinavia to perform "Parades and Changes."

Postpile on the eastern edge of the Sierra, Halprin suggests a building design reminiscent of those natural forms with an irregular, jagged perimeter and roof-line— not another faceless facade with a flat top. He also stresses the use of bay windows, one of the first uses of such window treatment incorporated into a high rise. The building's final design is altered as carried out. Skidmore, Owings & Merrill, executive architects. Completed 1972.

Custom House Plaza, Monterey, California. The challenge is to redevelop the oldest and most historic section of Monterey, the location of California's first state capital. Commissioned by the Monterey Urban Renewal Agency, the redevelopment plan specifies shops, motels, apartments, restaurants, offices, convention facilities, theaters, parking structures, a major department store, and improved traffic circulation. Halprin's landscape plan calls for the conversion of two main streets into pedestrian malls, with elevated walkways at second- and third-floor levels. Central to his plan are a large open-space plaza and a nearby park—both built atop a traffic tunnel. The overall plan contributes to the reestablishment of this historic center as the downtown nucleus. Wurster, Bernardi & Emmons, and Milton Schwartz & Associates, architects. Completed 1969.

Northpoint Apartments, San Francisco. Again with developer Gerson Bakar, Halprin carries out a project based on many of the design principles of the suburban Woodlake Apartments. This, however, is a very urban site covering three city blocks near Fisherman's Wharf and includes apartments, offices, and a shopping center. The overall design is that of a low-rise development based on inner courtyards with swimming pools, and roof-top gardens and terraces. Wurster, Bernardi & Emmons, architects. Completed 1967.

1965

May. Halprin serves as a panelist for the first "White House Conference on Natural Beauty" that helps to focus national attention on preserving the beauty of the American landscape. The conference leads to legislation requiring the future use of environmental-impact reports.

Travels throughout Scandinavia with his family and a group of teenagers as part of Dancers' Workshop, the theater/dance group founded by Anna Halprin. Uses scoring as a tool for choreographing a Dancers' Workshop performance entitled "Parades and Changes." Halprin is enormously affected by the character of Scandinavian new towns, their transportation systems, and the design of Tivoli Gardens in Copenhagen.

Serves as an advisor on the Board of Urban Consultants to the Federal Highway

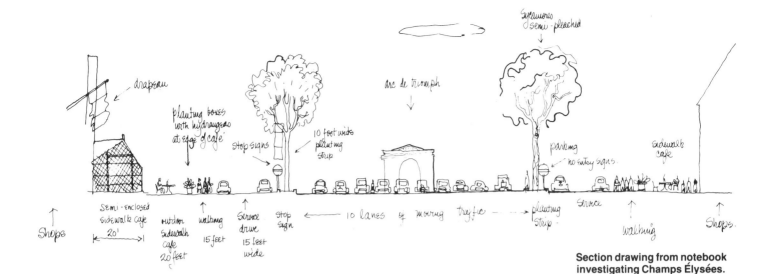

Section drawing from notebook investigating Champs Élysées.

Administrator, U.S. Bureau of Public Roads, establishing the esthetic potential of the freeway and its impact on cities. This represents the first time urban design principles, such as social impact and displacement of people, are applied to freeway design. Halprin maintains that these mammoth structures can do more than just function as transportation networks and can become forms of sculpture in the landscape, complementing rather than destroying the character of the cities they serve. The study ultimately results in the publication of *Freeways in the City,* a report to the U.S. Department of Transportation, which affects the future design of urban freeways.

Portland Open-Space Sequence, Portland, Oregon. This project represents a massive open-space network extending from Portland's downtown through the South Auditorium redevelopment area in a series of three one-acre plazas linked by walkways. Beginning at the waterfall and performance park, *Auditorium Forecourt* (now the *Ira Keller Fountain*), the fountain originates as a series of runnels that fall over twenty-foot concrete-block cliffs to a pool below. *Pettygrove Park* offers a contrasting spatial experience of green, grassy, high-rounded knolls, and trees. The sequence culminates in *Lovejoy Plaza,* a celebration of water and movement that resembles a piece of wilderness transplanted to the city. Active particpation in the fountain is the central theme inviting people in for wading and clambering and contemplation. The overall plan represents a microcosm of Halprin's notion of an ideal built environment as it threads its way through the city. Tree-lined walkways, which link the plazas, become a progression of fountains and places to sit.

Later in 1973, *Portland Transit Mall* is commissioned and encompasses thirteen blocks along two parallel streets. Transit is limited to bus and service-car access, while pedestrian use is unlimited. At each intersection, Halprin designs the pavement as a circular brick pathway, which enhances

The quiet elegance of Pettygrove Park.

Circular brick intersections celebrate the pedestrian at the Portland Transit Mall.

the sense of pedestrian crosswalks. Trees provide a canopy over widened sidewalks furnished with benches, kiosks, concessions, sculpture, fountains, and planters. Auditorium Forecourt, completed 1970, receives Smithsonian Institution Fifth Biennial HUD Award, Project Design, 1972; Pettygrove Park, completed 1966, receives American Association of Nurserymen, Commercial Landscaping Award, 1972; Lovejoy Plaza, completed 1966, receives Smithsonian Institution, 1968 Design Review, Industrial Design Award of Excellence; and Portland Transit Mall, completed 1978, receives AIA Award of Honor.

1966

Summer. *Workshop #1: "Experiments in Environment."* In Halprin's continuing search for new approaches to creativity, he organizes the first of four workshops devised to explore archetypal relationships between people and their environment. Held in the San Francisco Bay Area and on the northern California coast for a period of one month, he collaborates with Anna Halprin in the investigation of theories and approaches leading to integrated, cross-professional creativity. Architects, dancers, painters, landscape architects, and musicians take part in the workshop.

Appointed to the first National Council on the Arts by President Lyndon Baines Johnson, which, in its early years, establishes the basic premises for federal support for the arts in the United States. Serves through 1972.

Master Plan for Hadassah-Hebrew University Medical Center, Ein Karem, Israel. Devises a site plan for a complex of hospitals and medical schools where the famed Chagall stained-glass windows are located. The plan calls for extensive reforestation and conservation of the surrounding 340-acre site and for rebuilding the ancient walls and paths on a site a few miles outside Jerusalem. Joseph Neufeld, architect.

California State Fairgrounds Master Plan, Sacramento, California. Halprin's office and Wurster, Bernardi & Emmons act as coordinating architects for this 630-acre site on the American River. Built as the state's permanent fairgrounds, the master plan includes four major areas: a nine-acre exposition center, an activities complex, an industrial exhibit center, and a race track and recreational park. Waterways and overhead mini-rails traverse the site. Completed 1968.

Ida Crown Plaza, Israel National Museum, Jerusalem. The museum's main entrance plaza reflects a microcosm of the country's landscape: generally stark and multileveled, but occasionally bursting with color and splashing water. Olive, cedar, and other indigenous trees, plus the use of water in a system of man-made wells, jets, and cascades symbolize the more inviting aspects of the countryside. Within the plaza, water appears and disappears as it does in the mostly arid terrain of Israel. The plaza, donated by Chairman of the Board of General Dynamics, Henry Crown, in memory of his mother, is one of many projects supported by foreign contributions to the city of Jerusalem. Completed 1967.

Salk Institute for Biological Studies, La Jolla, California. Jonas Salk asks Halprin to study the original architectural design by Louis Kahn that calls for paved courtyards within the institute and to propose an alternate scheme. Halprin then redesigns the court-yards to include landscaped gardens. Kahn remains with his original plan for paved courtyards, and Halprin's design is eventually abandoned. Salk and Kahn, however, remain friends and colleagues as well as major influences in Halprin's life and career.

Appointed to first National Council on the Arts by President Lyndon Johnson.

Model of the California State Fairgrounds.

1967

September. Appointed by President Lyndon Baines Johnson to the first Advisory Council on Historic Preservation. Serves through 1970.

Corona/Flushing Meadow Sports Park, New York. Halprin is asked by Thomas Hoving, commissioner of the Parks, Recreational, and Cultural Affairs Administration of the City of New York, to develop a plan for a massive sports complex on the former 600-acre site of the 1939 and 1964 World's Fairs. This project is one of the first attempts to address issues of both active and passive recreation. In contrast to New York's Central Park, which was designed for the leisurely activities of strolling, sunning, and contemplating nature, Flushing Meadow emphasizes action and participation in all forms of sports. The complex is expected to draw people from the inner city as well as the outlying suburbs. One central concept of the plan is to have the park in use year-round, as well as all hours of the day and night. The team of Halprin, Kenzo Tange, and Marcel Breuer design the site with "something for everyone," with activities such as hopscotch, swimming, billiards, tennis, track, sledding, rock climbing, and camping, to name a few. Amenities such as restaurants, bars, hotels, and discotheques, along with a stadium and indoor basketball amphitheaters are also planned. Plan not implemented.

Jewish Home for the Aged, San Francisco. This garden is designed for the needs of the elderly. The lush, green, densely molded grounds provide areas for walking and convalescing, with sidewalks that are graded for wheelchairs and walkers. A gently tiered fountain/pool cuts into the sloping lawn, which can be viewed from the dining area. Chairs and benches are placed throughout. Howard Friedman, architect. Completed 1970.

Lake Merritt Channel Park, Oakland. Appointed by the City of Oakland and the Port of Oakland to convert a twenty-acre tract of inaccessible waterfront that lies between the Nimitz Freeway and the Oakland Estuary into a water-oriented park. The site becomes a focal point on a pedestrian promenade linking Lake Merritt to Jack London Square and emphasizes Oakland's ties to the sea by developing fish markets, fishing piers, and a small-boat harbor. Completed 1972.

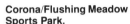

Halprin with Kenzo Tange and Marcel Breuer.

Corona/Flushing Meadow Sports Park.

The sculpted forms at the Jewish Home for the Aged.

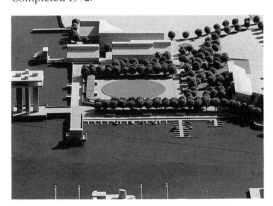

A water-oriented park between two freeways, the Lake Merritt Channel Park. Model.

Fully integrated planting, paving, and street furniture along Market Street.

Nasher Garden, an elegant residential garden.

Market Street, San Francisco. A major redesign project resulting from the 1962 report, "What To Do About Market Street?" Halprin's design interprets Market Street as a pedestrian-oriented sequence of open spaces with the street itself as the spine connecting them. *Embarcadero Plaza,* although not designed as part of this plan, acts as an anchor at the foot of Market Street. *Hallidie Plaza* is a sunken plaza incorporating a BART station and the terminus of the Powell Street cable car line. Further up the street is the *United Nations Plaza,* centering around a fountained environment that connects to a pedestrian mall leading to the civic center and city hall. Along the street are a variety of smaller plazas and alleyways with street furniture, sculpture, plantings, graphics, sidewalk widenings, and entrances to mass-transit systems. With John Carl Warnecke & Associates, and Mario Ciampi, architects. San Francisco Planning Director Alan Jacobs serves as an actively participating client. Completed 1970.

Nasher Garden, Dallas. Halprin designs this private garden as a series of outdoor "rooms," surrounding a fountain and swimming pool. One small room is left wild for the display of the owner's art collection, which includes pieces by artists such as Picasso, Joan Miró, Alberto Giacometti, Tony Smith, Henry Moore, and David Smith.

New York New York. A 119-page study commissioned by the City of New York that is actually a two-part presentation: the first is a series of proposals for reclaiming six urban renewal projects in the city; the second, a discussion of the quality, character, and meaning of open space in the urban environment—a complete course in the arcane mysteries of urban design. Issues such as housing, densities, zoning, and multi-dimensional systems of roof gardens and elevated walkways are emphasized. "The concept of involvement and participation underlies this whole report," says Halprin. "I'm beginning to see that the architect's job is basically to create spaces for people to be in, not buildings." This study is the first major proposal stressing the importance of citizens participating in what happens to, and in, their own environment. This concept of citizen's participation leads Halprin to his later Taking Part workshops. Completed 1968. Receives Smithsonian Institution, Industrial Design Award of Excellence, 1968; and Municipal Art Society of New York, Certificate of Merit, 1969.

1968

Anacostia River Master Plan, Washington, D.C. Sponsored by the National Park Service and the U.S. Department of Highways, this study results from Halprin's "Report to Mrs. Lyndon B. Johnson's Committee for a More Beautiful Capital." Halprin devises a plan that becomes an eleven-mile-long linear park bordering on a section of the Anacostia River that runs through ghettos and abandoned shipyards. Within the plan are recreational and cultural facilities such as small neighborhood museums and art centers, bike paths, a golf course, and a small ecological park. The study also provides alternate routes for the East Leg Freeway that had been previously scheduled to fill in much of the riverbed.

July. *Workshop #2: "Communities."* Halprin believes that the struggle in the creation of meaningful urban design is to find the right process of bringing together all the seemingly disparate elements and experiences that make up an urban environment. Hence, he organizes his second workshop for thirty students from a wide variety of disciplines for a month-long series of "Experiments in Environment."

Not the typical design seminar of lectures, slide presentations, and small group discussions, Halprin's classroom is in the field on Mount Tamalpais, at The Sea Ranch, and in San Francisco. These landscapes are to be evaluated through his more intuitive modes of perception, including kinesthetics, body participation, and other exploratory techniques of perception. Students are led on environmental-awareness walks in which they walk blindfolded, experiencing their surroundings by senses other than sight. Movement is investigated—dancers tell stories through motion, while architects create environments for them. Another experiment involves the construction of a driftwood village on a beach near The Sea Ranch. The only instructions are setting the center and bounds of the site and that there be no communication or collaboration between participants. After a day's work, a real "community" emerges with a gate, a main plaza, a tower, and individual houses. This workshop is a turning point in Halprin's approach to creativity and design, leading him to the synthesis of ideas and experiments that will later be published as *The RSVP Cycles: Creative Processes in the Human Environment.* With Anna Halprin and psychologist Paul Baum.

Virgin Islands Master Plan, St. Croix, St. John, and St. Thomas. In order to halt the haphazard development occurring throughout the American Virgin Islands, Halprin is asked by Secretary of the Interior, Stewart Udall, to draw up a conservation-oriented master plan with special emphasis on the waterfront in St. Thomas. Recommended in the plan are the use of cluster housing, moving the airport to the main island of St. Croix, and other aspects of limited development including tourism and industry. The project is terminated during the Nixon administration; however, some of the plan's recommendations are carried out.

Experiments in Environment, Workshop #2: "Communities."

1969

April. Halprin and other community members demonstrate for the preservation of Tamalpais Creek, a beautiful natural creek that runs through several communities in Marin County, California. The U.S. Army Corps of Engineers intends to transform "Tam" Creek into a flood-control channel by enlarging the creek bed, lining it with concrete, and then fencing off both sides. There is widespread opposition to the plan with Halprin drawing up less drastic and destructive alternative schemes. As a last resort, when all other compromises have failed, he and others lie down in front of the bulldozers to impede the work of the corps of engineers. All are arrested, and construction is subsequently completed.

June. Elected Fellow in The American Society of Landscape Architects.

Caracas Urban Plan, Caracas, Venezuela. Carlos Guinand Baldo, governor of the province and mayor of Caracas and himself an architect, commissions Halprin to study the "environmental future" of the city of Caracas. Halprin travels throughout Venezuela for several weeks and then develops studies, which include urban designs for the downtown core, open-space areas, parks and a new zoo, plazas and pedestrian walkways, and boulevards and transportation systems. Perhaps most significant are his studies of how to improve the slum areas, known as the barrios, by making them more healthful and livable. The studies are made with the collaboration of the distinguished Venezuelan architect

American Society of Landscape Architects.

Dr. Tomas Sanabria and results in a series of reports called "Caracas ¿Qué Pasa?" and "Caracas: Environmental Problems and Programs." Governor Baldo is not reelected to a following term and the proposals are not implemented.

Lawrence Halprin & Associates begins an innovative and extremely difficult process of intense reevaluation and restructuring of the firm. Reflecting the emerging social and political realities of the times—when resistance to the Vietnam War is reaching a crescendo and young people are increasingly voicing their dissent—the younger generation of employees is demanding more control in the day-to-day running of the office. Lawrence Halprin & Associates has grown to become a rather top-heavy

hierarchical organization with Halprin exercising total control. James Creighton, a communication psychologist, is asked to act as facilitator and open up communications between the differing groups. The firm, thereupon, embarks on a long series of weekly meetings, workshops, even a weekend retreat to The Sea Ranch. Everyone is encouraged to share their feelings, state their opinions, and, as a result, a small "revolution" occurs when Halprin is presented with an ultimatum to increase wages, distribute power, and acknowledge the importance of the younger generation in the office. In the end, Halprin maintains design authority, but the office is democratized. This rather difficult and harrowing approach to collective creativity is reported in *Innovation* and *Landscape Architecture* magazines.

Fort Worth Central Business District Master Plan, Fort Worth, Texas. The multi-use development plan of downtown Fort Worth evolves from participation of civic leaders in a Taking Part workshop. This process has been developed by Halprin to involve citizens and civic leaders in helping to shape their community's future. This first goal-oriented workshop (as opposed to the two earlier experiential workshops) uses the RSVP Cycles to determine and develop participant's ideas, goals, and attitudes toward their city. They first take sensitivity walks throughout downtown Fort Worth and then record their feelings and impressions through drawings. Though Halprin's master plan is not followed in detail, its basic principles have guided development of downtown Fort Worth ever since.

The Trinity River Report occurs as the result of the Fort Worth plan and addresses the eight-mile river loop through Fort Worth, proposing to convert the area to parks, hiking paths, picnic spots, and scenic areas. The U.S. Army Corps of Engineers had previously turned the banks into a river flood plan, causing the river to deteriorate. Halprin is called in by local citizens who want to rejuvenate the river, and work begins in 1976 on *Heritage Park,* located on the former site of a frontier fort. He proposes a series of low-level retention dams and a twelve-mile bike trail among picnic spots and scenic areas. Completed 1980.

Everett Community Plan and Report, Everett, Washington. Under a grant from the Federal Comprehensive Planning Act, Halprin is asked to develop an overall plan for a city suffering from years of uncontrolled growth and a dying urban core. He insists that the plan be the result of community involvement, not just the ideas of an uninvolved designer, who is not a member of their community. Several Taking Part workshops are held in which citizens express visions of their city's future and ways they can best be implemented. Completed 1973; receives HUD Design Award, 1974.

Heritage Park, a result of the Trinity River Report.

The talented and lively members of Lawrence Halprin & Associates.

Yerba Buena Center Master Plan and Report, San Francisco. Halprin is commissioned by the San Francisco Redevelopment Agency, and the City and County of San Francisco to devise a comprehensive master plan for the thirty-acre redevelopment site just south of Market Street. With Kenzo Tange & Urtec; McCue, Boone, Tomsick, architects. Not executed, but receives American Institute of Planners Merit Award for Environmental Design Excellence, 1970; and Fourth Biennial HUD Award, Urban Design Concept, 1970.

December. Mayor Teddy Kollek appoints Halprin to the Jerusalem Committee, an international, interfaith group engaged in ongoing dialog with the mayor about the future of Jerusalem on religious, sociological, cultural, planning, and architectural subjects. Continues to serve through 1986.

1970

Elected Honorary Fellow of The American Institute of Interior Design.

Seattle Freeway Park, Seattle. For the last fifteen years, Seattle's downtown freeway, Interstate 5, has cemented a division between the financial district and a residential neighborhood, keeping the two areas in total isolation from each other and carving a deep chasm through prime urban space. Due in part to Halprin's book, *Freeways,* published in 1966, the Seattle Park Commission contacts him for his ideas on developing an urban park on a proposed site adjoining the freeway. In an attempt to reconnect the two sections, Halprin makes an innovative proposal to the commission and convinces them to use the air rights over the interstate. His proposal is not only a first, but, by its implementation, enlarges the proposed park site and makes use of an otherwise unusable space. Even more space is acquired by utilizing the roof top of a proposed massive parking garage and a narrow strip of unused right-of-way land alongside an exit ramp. "The trick," says Halprin, "is to perceive the old freeway as a part of the cityscape and tame it, rather than to complain about it."

Water is used extensively throughout the design to drown out traffic noises. The focal point is a water canyon whose source is drawn from nature, but does not look natural. Gigantic planter boxes containing trees, which serve as visual backdrops and provide protection from wind and noise, are projected over the freeway. Freeway Park is one of Halprin's most influential urban design projects, demonstrating that usable, attractive spaces can be created from areas that were once believed to be of little or no use at all. Completed 1976. Receives *Design and Environment* magazine Award of Excellence, 1976; Association of Landscape Contractors of America, First Place Award, 1976; and American Society of Landscape Architects, Merit Award, 1977.

Seattle Freeway Park.

Skyline Park, Denver. This 3-block-long, 100-foot-wide linear park is the centerpiece of the "Skyline Denver" redevelopment program, itself a 113-acre, 27-block rejuvenation of downtown Denver. The park consists of a series of three plazas, each containing fountains and sculpture that invite active participation, as well as outdoor concerts and street fairs. Completed 1974; receives American Association of Nurserymen, Landscape Award, 1974.

Downtown Denver's linear Skyline Park.

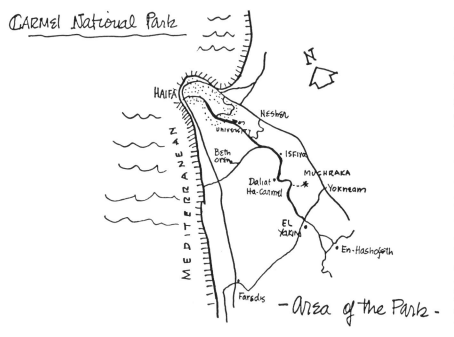

CARMEL National Park

HAIFA
Nesher
University
Beth oren
ISFIYA
MUCHRAKA
Daliat Ha-Carmel
Yokneam
EL YAKIN
En-Hashofeth
Faredis

MEDITERRANEAN

N

— Area of the Park —

Manhattan Square Park.

Willemstad Downtown Plan, Willemstad, Curaçao. The redevelopment of a small Dutch colonial island community off the coast of Venezuela whose downtown was destroyed following a riot. Halprin's plan calls for commercial development that is sensitive to both the island's historic atmosphere and the extraordinary natural beauty of the landscape. Completed 1971.

1971

March. Presents the annual lecture to the Royal Institute of British Architects. Rather than give a formal speech, Halprin produces the event as a theater piece with five players dressed in elegant costumes, who present the "lecture" for him. He writes each performer's score describing his urban designs and events occurring in them, and demonstrates how people can participate in activating their own city. The performance is choreographed with slides of Halprin's work.

Summer. Visits daughter Rana in Spain where she is studying flamenco dance at the Finca Espartero.

Workshop #3: "Leadership Training Workshop." After the 1966 and 1968 workshops, many former participants want to know how to run their own workshops. In this three-week-long session, Halprin trains thirty people in the processes of workshop facilitation . . . many of whom later conduct workshops as a profession.

Carmel National Park Master Plan and Report, Haifa, Israel. As consultant to the Israel National Park Service, Halprin calls for a plan that assures the continued existence of the area's natural environment. Besides the landscape, other already existing features— archeological digs, Druse villages, a quarry, and a rest home for a kibbutz—are maintained within the park.

Manhattan Square Park, Rochester, New York. Halprin is invited by the Rochester Redevelopment Agency to develop a five-acre park in a downtown area in need of revitalization. The park's central fountain cascades down concrete blocks whose forms are abstracted from nature, similar to the Lovejoy Fountain. This is perhaps his most multipurpose facility in that he takes the idea of a plaza one step further by extending it upward in the form of a space frame. A staircase within the frame permits the public to experience different levels and views. During concerts and plays in the 2,000-seat amphitheater, the space frame is used to support sound and lighting equipment. Completed 1976.

1972

March. Visits his daughter Daria Halprin, who is living in the Mabel Dodge Luhan House in Taos, New Mexico. Halprin is deeply moved and influenced by the Pueblo cultures and their integration of art, ritual, dance, and architecture as exemplified by the Taos pueblo.

May. Daria Halprin marries Dennis Hopper.

July. Participates in Doxiadis Conference held in Athens and on ships cruising the Greek Islands. Intellectuals are invited from all over the world to discuss issues of human settlements in the environment. From Halprin's notebook: "... the greatest combination of theater and discussion, intellect and diversity ... ongoing dialog in the mornings; island sails in the afternoons; festivities with the townspeople in the evenings ... intellectual activity combined with mystical, practical, and fantasy ... Herman Kahn standing at Delphi expounding on the future of mankind ... Margaret Mead, feisty and impetuous ... Jonas Salk, serious and inspiring ... Arnold Toynbee sitting on the steps of the Acropolis talking about the past and future ... Constantinos Doxiadis dancing with his granddaughter on the stage at Delphi ... Marshall McLuhan, tall and saturnine ... Buckminster Fuller, professing his child-like utopian vision of mankind ... Erik Erikson, bellyflopping into the sea ..."

December. First grandchild, Ruthanna, born to Daria and Dennis Hopper.

The Willamette Valley: Choices for the Future, Oregon. The 150-mile-long Willamette Valley stretches along the Willamette River between Portland and Eugene and is one of the richest agricultural and scenic areas in the country. Halprin is invited by Governor Tom McCall to explore the current problems of uncontrolled growth, which, if unchecked, will create a suburban corridor between the two cities. A Taking Part workshop is organized to involve residents in the decision making necessary for effecting the desired changes in their own environment. Halprin develops alternative scenarios in fifteen different categories— such as energy, transportation, and land use—that answer the questions, what kind of environment do you want to live in? and what sort of mechanisms can you use to control the economic and physical growth in your area *before* it's too late? The project results in a 115-page report presented to the Willamette Valley Environmental Protection and Development Council.

1973

August. Halprin opens a New York office in a historic building on Sniffen Court, which had been designed by Stanford White for the sculptor Malvina Hoffman.

Yountville Master Plan and Report, Yountville, California. A series of workshops are held locally to determine the ramifications of growth upon a small town in the wine country of the Napa Valley. Master-plan scenarios covering growth possibilities from no growth at all to uncontrolled, unlimited expansion are determined and then acted out by a Yountville theater group. Presented in this form, citizens are able to see, in an active multidimensional experience, the

HOpi → 1st mesa

Walpi pueblo - recall of the race at dawn up from the valley to the mesa - men on mesa call down encouragement & directions to the runners below who call back to them -- spectacular evocative relation both to environment & religion -- on mesa women wait with corn plants as part of the festive blessing...

Drawing of the pueblo, Taos, New Mexico, by Lawrence Halprin.

Yountville community in Napa Valley attending a workshop to discuss their community's future.

Ruthanna.

Located near the historic center of Cleveland is Settler's Landing. Model.

consequences of each scenario and decide which they prefer to follow.

Main Street Mall, Charlottesville, Virginia. Despite Charlottesville's historical legacy owing to Thomas Jefferson and his residence, Monticello, and the city's rich architectural history dating back to the American Revolution, its main street is declining with the advent of suburban shopping centers. This project represents the complete Halprin process in urban planning: first, he is invited by the city manager to give a Taking Part workshop; and, later, as a result of the workshop, carries out its consensus by designing a downtown pedestrian mall. Completed 1975.

A mall design as a result of a Taking Part workshop in Charlottesville, Virginia.

Corte Madera Creek, Greenbrae, California. A local citizen's group, led by Barbara Boxer, in opposition to the proposed development of a natural swamp-like area planned for condominiums, asks Halprin to conduct a workshop on the plan's feasibility. Workshop participants decide against development and by public pressure force the Marin County Board of Supervisors to buy the site and maintain it in its natural form.

Concept for Cleveland Master Plan, Cleveland. Relying heavily on citizen's participation through Taking Part workshops, Halprin's plan calls for the revitalizing of Cleveland's downtown core, particularly addressing Euclid Avenue from Public Square to Playhouse Square—the former being the city's symbolic, historical center, the latter its entertainment and commercial hub. Auto and transit loops are developed that will improve circulation, and twenty specific public improvements including malls, parks, city gateways, downtown housing, parking, a pedestrian bridge, and bus shelters are outlined. Completed 1976; receives *Design and Environment* magazine Award of Excellence, 1976.

In 1974, Halprin begins work on *Settler's Landing,* a mixed-use development located near Public Square. Included are a small hotel, boutique retail space, offices, museums, a riverfront promenade, and the renovation of a historic building originally designed by architect Daniel Burnham. Completed 1977.

Halprin is invited back in 1985 by the Cleveland Development Foundation to revisit the downtown area and give a critique of the progress that has been made in the years since the master plan's development.

1974

October. Originates *City Spirit* program for the National Endowment for the Arts, under the leadership of Chairperson Nancy Hanks. City Spirit is another of Halprin's investigations into the ongoing processes of creativity—an attempt to encourage and stimulate community organizations to create for themselves open forums on the use of art as creative forces in their communities. In 1975, after the formation of RoundHouse, Halprin conducts a Taking Part workshop in the Shenandoah National Park, Virginia, for a group of sixty professionals who will serve as City Spirit facilitators in communities throughout the United States.

November. *Federal Design Awareness Workshop,* Washington, D.C. Halprin is invited by Bill N. Lacy, director of the Department of Architecture and Environmental Arts Program at the National Endowment for the Arts, to coordinate and conduct a 2½-day workshop for representatives from each federal agency. The task-oriented mission of this workshop is to increase participant's appreciation and knowledge of design fundamentals, such as logo and publication design, and architectural and interior

space planning, with the ultimate goal of influencing the design standards of the federal government.

Virginia Museum of Art, Richmond, Virginia. For the museum's North Wing, Halprin designs a cascading fountain and pool as the central feature of a sculpture garden.

1975

With partner Sue Yung Li Ikeda, Halprin establishes RoundHouse, a studio/think-tank. Its intention is to explore modes of collective creativity; a search for collaborative processes by which groups of talented people in many fields can come together, evolving innovative solutions to significant issues through workshops, films, and designs. During the period of its existence, from 1975 through 1978, the following projects highlight their creative collaboration: *City Spirit Training Workshops* and the *Federal Design Awareness Workshop* for the National Endowment for the Arts (see October 1974), *Le Pink Grapefruit,* a film about Salvador Dali, (produced by Sue Yung Li Ikeda, directed by Lawrence Halprin), the *FDR Memorial* film (with Glen Fleck), the Report to Congress and the sculpture workshops, and *Workshop #4: Experiments in Environment.*

September. Travels with a group from RoundHouse to Cadaques, Spain, to make a film on Salvador Dali called *Le Pink Grapefruit.* The film is in preparation for Halprin's design of a proposed museum in Cleveland, Ohio, that will later house Dali's work. Also films and studies works of Antonio Gaudi in Barcelona.

1976

February–March. Solo exhibition at the San Francisco Museum of Modern Art, *Creative Processes in the Human Environment: Lawrence Halprin & Associates,* curated by Suzanne Foley, designed by Bruce Burdick.

Sue Yung Li Ikeda, Michael Lerner, and Halprin working on Round-House projects.

Takes a week-long trek by jeep through the Sinai from Sharm el Sheikh to St. Catherine's monastery. Climbs Mount Sinai and visits Bedouin encampments.

Franklin Delano Roosevelt Memorial, Washington, D.C. Following many years of intense controversy, heated competitions, and preliminary schemes, Halprin is commissioned by the Franklin Delano Roosevelt Memorial Commission to design a national memorial in his memory. The memorial is to be located on the Tidal Basin along the Cherry Walk between the Lincoln and Jefferson monuments. It is different from most monuments in that it is not an architectural design, but rather a landscape solution. Halprin attempts to secure an

A wall of water for FDR Memorial.
Model, Glen Fleck film.

integrated environment where people can be involved in many different qualities of experience—at times solemn and contemplative, but often joyful from the pure power derived from being within a peaceful and intricate garden. Halprin again choreographs movement as a central force in his design. The visitor is drawn from one area to another, for example, by the placement of a sculpture that is seen at first from a distance but is too small to be appreciated until up close, or by a flowery scent emanating from the other side of a wall. Water is a dominating factor in the plan—as it was in Roosevelt's life—with rivulets, jets, and planes of water

culminating at an amphitheater, which opens to the Tidal Basin.

Halprin selects the sculptors George Segal, Robert Graham, Leonard Baskin, and Neil Estern to collaborate with him in the representation of sequences from various periods of Roosevelt's presidency. A report on Halprin's design and a film by Glen Fleck are submitted to President Jimmy Carter in 1978. The design is approved in 1982 by the United States Congress and all relevant commissions, and signed into law by President Ronald Reagan. As of 1986, the memorial awaits construction funding from Congress.

San Fernando Arts Park, San Fernando Valley, California. In collaboration with architect Frank O. Gehry, Halprin devises a conceptual plan for an arts park, similar to Artpark in Lewiston, New York. Located on eighty acres of the Sepulveda Basin Recreation Park near the juncture of two freeways, it is to be an alternative space for filmmakers, musicians, poets, architects, sculptors, and dancers to develop their art forms. For the public, art is to be presented as a kind of recreation. The park features both formal and informal spaces such as an outdoor amphitheater, performance pavilion, theaters, galleries, and studio spaces. Not implemented.

Disbands firm of Lawrence Halprin & Associates. Although the group has been brought together over the years as a talented and innovative environmental design/ planning office, it has grown to almost sixty members, with Halprin becoming increasingly insulated from the hands-on, day-to-day creative involvement in developing new approaches to design, which

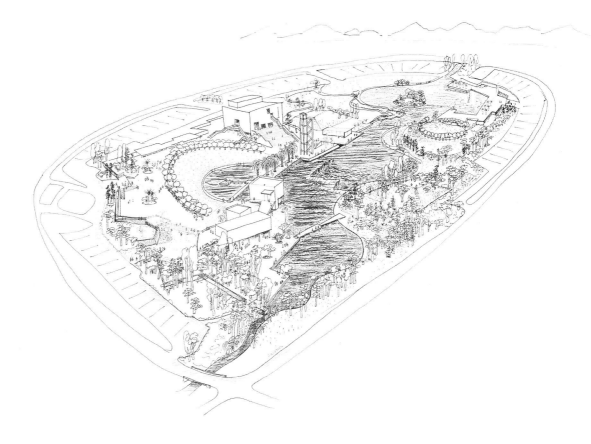

Designed with Frank O. Gehry, an overview of the proposed San Fernando Arts Park.

lay at the core of his artistic interests. In departing from his large office practice, he turns his energies full time to RoundHouse.

1977

Workshop #4: "Experiments in Environment." Produced for the College of Environmental Design, University of California, Berkeley, the workshop explores the essence of the person/environment relationship. The ten-day workshop for twenty-eight students takes place in San Francisco and at The Sea Ranch, and reveals some rather unexpected archetypal themes in the human environment. One experiment leads participants in exploring such basic forces in the cosmos as life and death. In the Chinese concept of the universe, people can either impede or improve these cosmic forces, so it follows that they need to be understood for all life's activities. For example, when people modify the land and build upon it, these forces are consulted to guide the planning of buildings and gardens. This is "Fung Sui" or the ancient Chinese art of geomancy. On a ridge overlooking the ocean at The Sea Ranch, participants in this score are to search out and find their spot of life and their spot of death. For a few, this turns out to be one and the same place; however, most choose two greatly contrasting settings. One person's discovery: "A comfortable death-place in the redwoods, amid decay and new growth. For life, I want an open landscape, warmed by the sun, looking out over everything."

In another experience revealing archetypal themes, it is discovered that significant group differences emerge between male and female approaches to their environment. In an event on a beach-front site, women first explore individually, looking at, sensing, and feeling the area. Eventually, without signal, they come together into a hollow formed by cypress trees. There they sit in the womb-like enclosure—protected, relating to one another, warm, friendly, laughing. The men, on the other hand, march into the site in a column and together traverse it—determined, solemn, wary, somber. They end up on a high knoll from which they can visually dominate the entire site, including the women in their hollow below. *A Report on TAKING PART at CED* is produced as a result of this workshop.

1978

June. Reopens Lawrence Halprin design firm in San Francisco as a small group dedicated to creative design in the environment.

September. Elected to The American Academy of Arts and Sciences.

September. Rana Halprin marries Jasper Vassau.

November. Awarded The American Society of Landscape Architects Gold Medal.

Ten-day "Experiments in Environment" to explore basic forces in the cosmos.

Death Place: A high, rounded hillside, buffeted by wind, a limitless horizon, the sun's setting rays.

Hugh granite from the High Sierra is the focal point of Levi's Plaza.

Serves on the advisory panel to the School of Fine Arts of the American Academy in Rome.

Levi's Plaza, San Francisco. The process whereby Levi Strauss, Inc., arrives at this campus-like setting, with its corporate headquarters tucked into the foot of Telegraph Hill, is an interesting one in itself. After outgrowing its original 1906 building, the corporation established itself into many floors of a modern San Francisco high rise. Once moved, however, they found their new environment destroying their more casual, family-style existence and decide to build their own headquarters—not in the suburbs where many businesses are going, but in the city.

The new quarters are several buildings, from four to ten stories high, set amid plazas and parks. Sheltered from the traffic running along The Embarcadero, with views of the Bay beyond, the site is designed by Halprin as a place for employees to lunch, relax in and around their place of work, and to maximize interaction between workers. There are two distinct parts of the park, each providing different environments. The plaza is an urban space and becomes the focal point of the surrounding buildings, with a fountain utilizing a single, massive piece of carnelian granite. The park's east side, which is separated from the buildings by a street, features a meandering stream and a cascading waterfall surrounded by grassy knolls and pathways. With architects Hellmuth, Obata & Kassabaum, and Gensler & Associates. Completed 1982.

Halprin's studio at The Sea Ranch.

Levanna.

1979

January. RoundHouse is formally dissolved.

May–August. Included in group exhibition at the California Academy of Sciences, San Francisco, *Creativity: The Human Resource,* designed by The Burdick Group and sponsored by Chevron. The show travels nationally and goes on permanent display at the Pacific Science Center in Seattle.

April. Awarded the Thomas Jefferson Gold Medal in Architecture by University of Virginia, Charlottesville.

RSVP Cycles Training Workshops, Japan. Halprin agrees to conduct a workshop for the Tokyu Company's management-level personnel if an additional workshop can likewise be held for artists. The artist's workshop, consisting of painters, writers, academicians, architects, and landscape architects, is held in Hakone, a historic lake resort near Mount Fuji that serves as a pastoral setting for exploring creative processes. In contrast to the Hakone workshop, the management-training workshop takes place in the dense, urban Tamagawa section of Tokyo, and trains the professional members of the Tokyu Company in the Taking Part processes as they relate specifically to the company. As a result of this interaction, several participants apply the workshop process to their individual business. Jim Burns and Anna Halprin, participating faculty.

November. Second granddaughter, Levanna Vassau, born to Rana and Jasper Vassau.

December. Daria Halprin Hopper marries Khosrow Khaligi.

Halprin Studio, The Sea Ranch, California. Designs and builds a twenty-foot-cube studio as his own personal design and painting retreat.

Charles Moore and Halprin collaborate to design part of the ambitious and daring plan for the Bunker Hill Competition.

Armon Hanatziv Master Plan, Jerusalem. Many Jerusalemites regard this as Halprin's finest contribution to their city. In essence it preserves the magnificent views of the Old City, looking from the crest of the Kidron Bowl that extends from the Armon Hanatziv (the "High Commissioner's Castle") to Abu Tor. Halprin's master plan calls for using only infill housing to halt the suburbanization process, keeping the existing roadways, planning a promenade on a surrounding ridge, preserving the remaining open space in the basin, maintaining planting appropriate to the area, and providing recreation, such as hiking and picnic facilities. Completed 1981.

Ben Yehuda Street Studies, Jerusalem. Like main streets everywhere, this main shopping street of downtown Jerusalem offers all the typical noise and traffic congestion. In its place, Mayor Teddy Kollek conceives of a pedestrian mall lined with shops, sidewalk cafés, and restaurants and asks Halprin to design it. After completion, the area becomes one of the city's most vibrant sections, providing and encouraging street life . . . especially for Jerusalem's younger population.

1980

February–April. Solo exhibition, *Lawrence Halprin: Concepts,* curated by Charles Moore for University of California, Los Angeles, Architecture Department.

June–July. Solo exhibition, *Lawrence Halprin: Paintings, Drawings, and Design Sketches,* Philippe Bonnafant Gallery, San Francisco.

November–December. Solo exhibition, *Lawrence Halprin, Landscape Sketches,* SPACED: Gallery of Architecture, New York.

Bunker Hill Competition, Los Angeles. The project, a major mixed-use development competition sponsored by the Los Angeles Community Redevelopment Agency, includes four office towers, a hotel, and a new Museum of Contemporary Art. The concept of putting together an extraordinary group of international design talent is conceived by Maguire Thomas Partners. This particular team includes Barton Myers, Harvey Perloff, Edgardo Contini, Cesar Pelli, Lawrence Halprin, Charles Moore, Robert Kennard, Ricardo Legorreta, Hugh Hardy, and Frank O. Gehry. Their proposal is the creation of an intense urban experience for the city— a totally new civic experience. Although this proposal is widely acclaimed, it does not win the competition, but it has a vitalizing effect on city imagery through wide publication.

Pioneer Square Competition, Portland, Oregon. The site is a downtown city block used as a two-level parking garage opposite the Pioneer Courthouse. It is generally felt by many community groups and city agencies that the block is too valuable for parking. Under the sponsorship of the Portland

Development Commission, a competition is held for its conversion into a public plaza. With Charles Moore, Halprin devises a scheme containing a watergarden that originates in a grotto under the stage and cascades down into a series of terraced pools. When the water is turned off, the garden becomes a central stage surrounded by seating. A glass atrium-like structure housing an interior wintergarden with cafés, restaurants, and an information center complete the major elements of the scheme. Not implemented.

Yerba Buena Gardens and Master Plan, San Francisco. This project, located on the original site of the unbuilt Yerba Buena Center in the heart of downtown, is a twenty-four-acre plot designated for cultural, recreation, entertainment, and commercial activities, with ten acres devoted to open space and gardens. Sponsorship is under the San Francisco Redevelopment Agency and guided by a development team including Olympia & York, the Marriott Corporation, and Beverly A. Willis. An esplanade and Grand Fountain for performances and public events are incorporated into the preliminary plan by Halprin, plus small gardens including a learning garden, a children's garden, and a classical Chinese garden designed in cooperation with San Francisco's sister city, Shanghai. With architects Zeidler Roberts Partnership.

The Rovah Buildings and Garden, Jerusalem. The site lies within an area of the Old City known as the Jewish Quarter that was largely reduced to rubble after the 1948 War of Independence, and occupied by Jordan until the 1967 Six Day War when Israel regained the area. Halprin's rebuilding program includes an underground entrance tunnel into the Old City (thereby preserving the ancient city wall), a bus terminal, a four-level sub-surface parking garage, new housing units, commercial space with cafés and restaurants, an archeological garden to preserve and give access to excavations and recently uncovered Byzantine churches, and a series of plazas, paths, and walkways. The intent is to maintain the esthetic and Biblical integrity of the Old City, while incorporating elements of the modern.

1981

January—May. With Anna Halprin and her Tamalpa Institute, Halprin conducts a series of lectures and workshops entitled "Searching for Living Myths and Rituals."

March. Third grandchild, Jahan, born to Daria and Khosrow Khaligi.

April. Delivers Frederick Law Olmsted Lecture, "Creativity in Landscape Architecture," at Harvard University, Cambridge, Massachusetts. In his lecture, Halprin discusses creativity in shaping the environment, the theory of experiential equivalency, and the search for modern myths.

Sketch from the Yerba Buena Gardens Master Plan. Drawing by Lawrence Halprin.

Jahan (J.J.).

A driftwood village created by students in the "LA Spectacular" workshop.

Workshop #5: "LA Spectacular." Halprin conducts a weekend workshop for a class of Charles Moore's graduate students from the University of California, Los Angeles, Architecture Department. The intent of the workshop is to explore the essence of architecture on its most primitive level. Students spend a day together on a beach at The Sea Ranch, silently, with no communication among themselves, building a community out of driftwood and other natural materials found on the site. The group's construction reveals many of the archetypal elements of a basic city plan: a center, a sacred space, pathways, and housing around a strong geometric core.

November. Invited by the Royal Institute of Architects and sponsored by the Architecture and Design Committee of the Arts Council of Australia to give a three-week series of lectures and workshops entitled "Art of the Environment" in Perth, Melbourne, and Sydney.

March—April. Concurrent one-person exhibition, *A Seamless Whole,* at the Gund Hall Gallery, Harvard University Graduate School of Design. Shown is a collection of Halprin's paintings, drawings, and sketches, which later travel nationally.

April—May. Solo exhibition, *Design Sketches, Recent Projects,* Philippe Bonnafant Gallery, San Francisco.

Travels with daughter Rana and son-in-law Jasper to Santa Fe, New Mexico, to witness Walpi and Hopi snake dances.

Crocker Court, Los Angeles. On a site between the Crocker Towers, designed by Skidmore, Owings & Merrill, Halprin creates a sort of urban, indoor Garden of Eden. Trees and shrubs are planted in different sizes and in different scales to one another, with the intent of producing for the viewer the illusion of not knowing the true size of anything. Robert Graham is commissioned by Halprin to create three sculptures as centerpieces for the fountains that are connected together by runnels. The fountains and runnels provide the constant sounds of running water throughout the gardens. His multiple sculptures of the same human figure, each posed in a different athletic stance, are also off-scale and smaller than life size, adding further to the feeling of fantasy. Completed 1983.

Crocker Court, the interior atrium of Crocker Towers.

Bronze sculpture by Robert Graham.

Raymer Garden.

Halprin sketching at the
Grand Canyon.

Raymer Garden and Guest House, Atherton,
California. This commission represents the
first private garden Halprin has executed in
twenty years. The design emphasizes use of
strong colors in the densely wooded site. The
swimming pool tile, fence, trellis, and
plantings are all developed from a vibrant
palette. Completed 1984.

1982

July. Presents lecture, "Design Process for
Levi's Park and Plaza," at Stanford Conference
on Design, Stanford University, Stanford,
California.

October. Presents lecture, "Environmental
Empathy," at High Museum of Art, Atlanta.

Travels with anthropologist Edward T. Hall on
camping trip through Arizona and New
Mexico, visiting Canyon de Chelly National
Monument, Anasazi historical ruins, and
Navajo and Hopi villages where Halprin
studies the relation of indigenous architecture
to Native American myths and rituals.

Holocaust Memorial Competition, San
Francisco. The essence of the memorial's
design is to create an experience in which
visitors can have the opportunity to meditate
and reflect on the horror of the Holocaust
and, thus, on the meaning of life itself. With
sculptor Robert Graham, Halprin conceives
of the spiral, a form that exemplifies to
Halprin growth and change, and through
which participants gradually descend into a
pitted area representing isolation, horror,
evil. From here, one begins the upward
ascent through a tunnel whose walls are
inscribed with quotations from victims of the
death camps. Visitors emerge from the
tunnel's darkness into sunlight and cypress
trees, offering hope for the future of
mankind. Commissioned and funded by
Mayor Feinstein's Committee for a Memorial
. . . and the Jewish Community Relations
Council. Not implemented.

1983

February. Appointed Regents Lecturer for
one year at the University of California,
Berkeley, School of Environmental Design.
Delivers several lectures on the "emotional
landscape."

Visits the Flying X Ranch in Forsyth, Montana,
home of son-in-law Jasper's family. Also visits
the Native American reservation, Lame Deer.

October—November. Group exhibition, *The
Sea Ranch: Building for the Landscape,* at
the AIA San Francisco Gallery. Group
includes Halprin, Esherick, Moore, Lyndon,
Turnbull, and Whitaker.

November. Lectures on the Franklin Delano
Roosevelt Memorial, in conjunction with the
"Competitions Won and Lost" lecture series,
sponsored by the San Francisco Museum of
Modern Art and The American Institute of
Architects.

Halprin begins a series of workshops that
lead to *Designed Environments for
Everyone,* a film about how to design for the
disabled, produced by Michael Lerner.

Conducts a series of workshops for
homeowners at The Sea Ranch entitled, "The
Sea Ranch, Process for the Future." Twenty
years have passed since the development's
inception, and a sense of loss of the original
intent is becoming apparent. Over a period
of several weekends, 300 to 400 homeowners participate in rededicating themselves
to the early philosophy of The Sea Ranch.

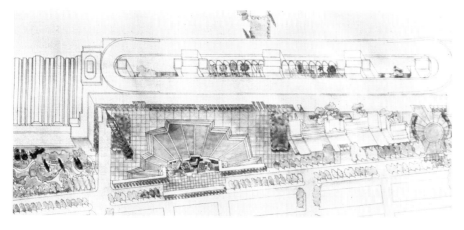

Plan of the Lingotto Factory.

The famed Lingotto Factory, the subject of a prototype Taking Part workshop.

Bunker Hill Steps.

Lingotto Factory, Turin, Italy. A roof-top race track crowns this half-mile-long automobile factory, designed in 1916 by Giacomo Matté Trucco. Recently abandoned due to outdated technology, Fiat commissions twenty internationally acclaimed architects to come up with solutions for the building's reuse. The project is conducted not in the spirit of a competition, but rather as an evolution of ideas that will preserve the building but alter its outdated function. Halprin's idea is to involve the citizens of Turin in the decision-making process. In order to graphically demonstrate this concept, he conducts a prototype Taking Part workshop in San Francisco in which several schemes are actually developed for the factory. The videotaped workshop is then displayed in Turin, along with presentation drawings that show the factory and its site recycled as housing, museums, shopping arcades, a children's park and playground, and a great plaza for city-wide events.

Plaza Las Fuentes, Pasadena, California. Reaching back to the bungalow-style houses designed by Pasadena architects Charles and Henry Green in the early 1900s and inspired by the Mediterranean gardens of Spain and Italy, this mixed-use development next to Pasadena's Civic Center strives to express both a historical and regional character. With architects Moore, Ruble & Yudell, and developers Maguire Thomas Partners.

Los Angeles Open-Space Network is a series of independent projects involving steps, streets, gardens, and parks in downtown Los Angeles, under the aegis of the Los Angeles Community Redevelopment Agency. Together, these projects represent a concerted attempt to make downtown Los Angeles an accessible and also pleasing experience for pedestrians.

Bunker Hill Steps is a grand stairway and watergarden, reminiscent of Rome's Spanish Steps, which will link the traditional downtown to the newly developed Bunker Hill section. Halprin choreographs the steps as an urban experience not unlike that of a city street. A "museum wall," displaying sculpture grottoes, frescoes, and fountains, bounds the steps on one side while, on the other, it curves around a seventy-story high rise currently being designed by I.M. Pei & Partners. Terraced landings, retail shops, and outdoor cafés offer a choice of activities for relaxing, lunching, or shopping. At the top of the steps is a fountain that sends runnels meandering down through the middle of the grand stairway. With developers Maguire Thomas Partners. Projected completion 1987.

Halprin is commissioned to design the Los Angeles *Library Gardens* on a site that adjoins the central library and is currently being used as a parking lot. The library was originally designed by Bertram Goodhue in 1926 and is undergoing restoration and remodeling by architects Hardy, Holzman & Pfeiffer. The gardens will be linked to the

Bunker Hill Steps by a pedestrian mid-block crossing. With developers Maguire Thomas Partners. Projected completion 1988.

Olympic Park will serve as a gateway to South Park, a developing residential, cultural, and commercial district in southeast downtown Los Angeles. Halprin's plan for this new four-acre neighborhood park includes a plaza, fountains, gardens, an arcade and will incorporate housing and a new campus for the Fashion Institute of Design and Merchandising. Projected completion 1987.

Along a ten-block section of *Hope Street,* Halprin is creating a master plan calling for the widening and repaving of sidewalks, providing areas for street furniture, and devising a landscape plan for trees and other plantings. This section of Hope Street will be a pedestrian-oriented connector between the Library Gardens and Olympic Park. Projected completion 1987.

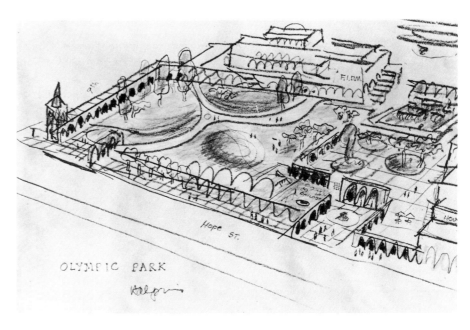

A new four-acre Olympic Park on Hope Street.

1984

September. Joins son-in-law Jasper and his family in a week-long overland expedition via wagon train between Forsyth and Miles City, Montana, in celebration of the 100th anniversary of Miles City.

The Westchester Wall, Los Angeles. Near the intersection of the San Diego Freeway and Sepulveda Boulevard, the three-quarter-mile-long wall forms a parklike edge for the first phase of the Howard Hughes Center —a seventy-acre mixed-use development. Designed by Halprin as a sequence of walls, terraces, and towers, which mask noise from the nearby roadways, the wall's colors and textures relate back to early southern California architecture. Completed 1985.

Walter and Elise Haas Promenade, Jerusalem. Almost a mile in length, the promenade stretches along the top of a ridge, overlooking the Biblical landscape of the Old City. Within Halprin's plan are places for viewing, sitting, and strolling, with descriptive posts identifying points of interest. Niches in a wall paralleling the promenade hold various archeological artifacts. At one end of the promenade is a belvedere with café, bar, and terrace overlooking the city. Local Jerusalem stone is used throughout. Projected completion 1986.

Sea Ranch Professional Consultation Group. As a result of the 1983 workshop, "The Sea Ranch, Process for the Future," it was determined that a new group of interested professionals should be brought together with the original Sea Ranch design team to devise a new set of guidelines for the next twenty years. This team, known as the Professional Consultation Group, consists of Al Boeke, Joseph Esherick, Charles Moore, William Turnbull, Donald MacDonald, Reverdy Johnson, Jack Cosner, Hideo Sasaki, and Lawrence Halprin. The group concludes that problems lay not so much in individual house design, but the way in which, in more recent years especially, they have been laid upon the land. The group's first priority is to develop a new environmental plan that takes into consideration all the changes that have taken place since The Sea Ranch was founded. A report, "Design Guidelines for the Future," is produced by Jim Burns and Duane Gordon.

1985

October. Presents lecture, "What Makes Cities Liveable?" for the Oregon Historical Society, Portland, Oregon.

June. Halprin participates in The International Forum on the Future of Sam Rodia's Towers in Watts.

July. Receives the San Francisco Arts Commission Award of Honor in Landscape Architecture.

December. Travels to Israel to begin open-space master-plan studies for the city of Eilat, on the Gulf of Aquaba, and the village of Lifta, dating back to Biblical times. At Lifta, Halprin has been commissioned by Mayor Teddy Kollek to act as design consultant in the planning of a nature reserve headquarters, museum, and study center.

1986

April. Receives the Richard Neutra Award for professional excellence, given by the School of Environmental Design at California State Polytechnic University, Pomona.

July. *Lawrence Halprin: Changing Places* opens at the San Francisco Museum of Modern Art. The exhibition is curated by Helene Fried and designed by Frank O. Gehry, with a catalog edited by Lynne Creighton Neall and designed by Suzanne Anderson-Carey.

Selected Bibliography

Books

Brambilla, Roberto, and Gianni Longo. *What Makes Cities Liveable: Learning From Seattle.* National Endowment for the Arts, 1979.

Burns, Jim. *Lawrence Halprin Paesaggista.* Edited by Bruno Zevi. Bari, Italy: Edizione Dedalo, 1982. (Italian text, English insert available.)

The Franklin Delano Roosevelt Memorial, A Report to Congress by RoundHouse for the FDR Memorial Commission. May 1978.

G.A. Document: Special Issue 1970–1980. A.D.A. Edita Tokyo Company, Inc., 1980.

Halprin, Lawrence. *Cities.* rev. ed. Cambridge: MIT Press, 1972.

_____. "The Collective Perception of Cities." Edited by Lisa Taylor. *Urban Open Spaces.* New York: Rizzoli, 1981.

_____. *Freeways.* New York: Reinhold Publishing, 1966.

_____. *New York New York.* Department of Housing and Urban Development, and the New York Foundation, 1968.

_____. *RSVP Cycles: Creative Processes in the Human Environment.* New York: George Braziller, 1970.

_____, et al. *The Freeway in the City.* Washington, DC: Government Printing Office, 1968.

_____, and Jim Burns. *Taking Part: A Workshop Approach to Collective Creativity.* Cambridge: MIT Press, 1974.

_____. "The RSVP Cycles." Edited by James C. Budd. *Juxtapositions.* Palo Alto, California: Science Research Associates, 1971.

_____. "The Creative Approach to a Quality Environment." Edited by Harold Helfrinch, Jr. *Agenda for Survival: The Environmental Crisis.* New Haven: Yale University Press, 1970.

_____. "The Landscape Architect and the Planner." Edited by Sylvia Crowe. *Space For Living.* Amsterdam: Djambatan Publishers and Cartographers, 1961.

_____. "The Meaning of Communications." Edited by Robert Haigh. *Communication in the 21st Century.* New York: John Wiley & Sons, 1981.

_____. "Urban Rituals." Edited by Lisa Taylor. *Cities: The Forces that Shape Them.* New York: Cooper-Hewitt Museum, 1982.

Lingotto: Venti Progetti per II Futuro del Lingotto. Milano: Gruppo Editoriale Fabbri-Bompiani, Sonzogno, Etas S.p.A., 1984.

National Endowment for the Arts: City Spirit Facilitation. San Francisco: RoundHouse, 1976.

Notebooks of Lawrence Halprin, 1959–1971. Cambridge: MIT Press, 1972.

Process Architecture Number Four, Lawrence Halprin. Tokyo: Process Architecture Publishing Co. Ltd., 1978.

Sketchbooks of Lawrence Halprin. Toyko: Process Architecture Publishing Co. Ltd., 1981.

Take Part. By Lawrence Halprin & Associates. Portland, Oregon: Portland Press, 1972.

Journal Articles

Aidala, Thomas. "The FDR Memorial: Halprin Redefines the Monumental Landscape." *Landscape Architecture,* January 1979, 42–52.

"An Architect Who Builds for People." *San Francisco Sunday Examiner,* 23 April, 1972, 17.

Bennett, Richard. "Random Observations on Shopping Centers and Planning for Pedestrians." *Architectural Record,* September 1957, 217–28.

Breckenfield, Gurney. "The Odyssey of Levi Strauss." *Fortune,* 22 March 1982, 110.

Buel, Ronald A. "The Halprin Experience." *San Francisco Magazine,* March 1968.

_____. "Shaping Cities." *The Wall Street Journal,* 8 June 1967.

Burns, Jim. "Century 21 Seattle 1962 World's Fair." *Progressive Architecture,* June 1962, 49–64.

_____. "Marschrichtung: Einbeziehung der Betroffenen." *Garten und Landschaft,* August 1975, 504–11.

_____. "Experiments in Environment." *Progressive Architecture,* July 1967.

_____. "Sea Ranch: Resisting Suburbia." *Architecture,* December 1984, 56–63.

"By Passed Land." *House and Home,* February 1957, 108–15.

"Candlestick Park Looks Worse Than a Prison." *San Francisco Chronicle,* 21 November 1961.

Canty, Donald. "Market Street, San Francisco." *AIA Journal,* August 1980, 32–46.

_____. "Corporate Campus Laid Back Against Telegraph Hill." *AIA Journal,* May 1982, 152–59.

Carter, Malcolm. "The FDR Memorial: A Monument to the Art of Accommodation." *Artnews,* October 1978, 50–57.

Cohen, Paul. "A Sketch in Time." *New West,* 30 June 1980, 23–24.

"The Compartmented House." *House and Garden,* August 1962, 67–73.

"A Condominium Castle for Weekend Living." *Fortune,* May 1966, 135–37.

Davis, Douglas. "Planning Spaces for People, Not Buildings." *The National Observer,* 23 June 1969.

_____. "Spaces for our Time." *Newsweek,* 24 December 1973, 76–79.

Drossel, Margaret. "Cities Don't Have to Be Ugly." *Engineering News Record,* 7 November 1968, 53–55.

"Ecological Architecture: Planning the Organic Environment." *Progressive Architecture,* May 1966, 120–134.

"FDR and the Cherry Blossoms." *Horizon,* May 1977, 57–61.

Foote, Nancy. "Sightings on Siting." *Art, Architecture, Audience: Urban Encounters*, March–April 1980, 32.

Freeman, Adele. "Halprin Wants Architecture with All-Around Sensual Appeal." *The Globe and Mail* (Toronto), 17 October 1981, 5.

Frey, Susan Rademacher. "Proposal for a Holocaust Memorial." *Landscape Architecture*, March–April 1984, 52–55.

"Golden Gate Theological Seminary." *Architectural Record*, August 1957, 148–151.

Goldstein, Barbara. "Participation Workshops." *Architectural Design*, April 1974, 207–212.

Gray, Christopher. "The Sea Ranch." *House and Garden*, September 1985.

Halprin, Lawrence. "The Art of Garden Design." *Journal Royal Architectural Institute of Canada*, July 1954, 226–27.

_____. "The Choreography of Gardens." *Impulse*, 1949, 30–34.

_____. "The City Tree." *Architectural Forum*, October 1961, 134–39.

_____. "The Community in the Landscape." *AIA Journal*, September 1961, 52–57.

_____. "Dance Deck in the Woods." *Impulse*, 1956, 21–23.

_____. "The Gardens of the High Sierra." *Landscape*, Winter 1961–1962, 26–28.

_____. "How to Score." *RIBA Journal*, July 1971, 290–94.

_____. "Israel: New Life for an Old Land." *Landscape Architecture*, April 1962, 1–4.

_____. "Jerusalem As Place and Vision." *AIA Journal*, December 1980, 32–37.

_____. "Landscape Between Walls." *Architectural Forum*, November 1959, 148–153.

_____. "The Last Forty Years: A Personal Overview of Landscape Architecture in America." *Space Design: Gardens, Wonderland of Contrivance and Illusion*, April 1984, 5–7.

_____. "Lawrence Halprin on Freeways." *Architecture/West*, July 1965.

_____. "Motation." *Progressive Architecture*, July 1965, 126–133.

_____. "The Shape of Erosion." *Landscape Architecture*, January 1962, 87–88.

_____. "Why I'm in Favor of the Panhandle Freeway." *San Francisco Examiner*, 3 May 1964.

Huxtable, Ada Louise. "Nobody Here But Us New Yorkers." *The New York Times*, 19 May 1968.

"The Kentfield Home of the Halprins: A Dwelling Built for a Dancer." *San Francisco Chronicle*, 26 July 1959.

Knight, Pamela. "Shelters on a Scalloped Shore." *Sports Illustrated*, 28 March 1966, 46–52.

Koolhaus, Rem. "Arthur Erikson vs. the All Stars: The Battle of Bunker Hill." *Trace*, July-September 1981, 9–15.

Lawrence Halprin in Australia." *Landscape Architecture* (Australia Institute of Landscape Architects), February 1982, 29–35.

Leefe, James M. "Ghirardelli Square." *Interiors*, October 1965, 98–109.

Lipton, Lenny. "The Surrealist Shooting of 'Le Pink Grapefruit.'" *American Cinematographer*, March 1977, 306–07.

Lloyd-Jones, David. "Lawrence Halprin: Eco-Architect." *Horizon*, Summer 1970, 46–55.

Lindgren, Nilo. "A Radical Experiment in Reorganization." *Innovations*, No. 18, 1971, 46–60.

_____. "Riding a Revolution Part I: A Radical Experiment in Reorganization Part II: Halprin Revisited in 1973." *Landscape Architecture*, April 1974, 133–47.

Lyndon, Donlyn. "Concrete Cascade in Portland." *Architectural Forum*, August 1966, 74–79.

McHarg, Ian. "Three Essays on Urban Space." *Art, Architecture, Audience: Urban Encounters*, March–April 1980, 21–24.

Miller, Betty. "Urban Forestry West: Seattle's Freeway Park." *American Forest*, October 1979, 29–31.

Mlachak, Norman. "Halprin 'Playshop' Grads May Save City." *The Cleveland Press*, 14 August 1975, A4.

Nairn, Janet. "Building Type Studies, Low Rise Office Buildings: Levi's Plaza." *Architectural Record*, May 1982, 114–19.

"Newest City Parks Dedicated with Toss of Historic Coin." *The Oregonian*, 27 July 1966, 14.

"Office and Warehouse for Parke Davis." *Architectural Record*, June 1959, 175–182.

Pastier, John. "A Grand Avenue." *A+U*, August 1981, 44–45.

_____. "Evaluation: Park Atop a Freeway." *AIA Journal*, June 1983, 43.

Peter, John. "California: Second Homes Spare the Land." *Look*, 28 June 1966, 84–85.

"Piazza di Kansas City." *Progressive Architecture*, July 1966, 163–65.

"Planning Life on a 55-foot Lot." *Sunset*, January 1948, 16–19.

Platt, Bill. "The Sea Ranch as International Community." *Ridge Review*, Fall 1983, 13–20.

"Portrait of a Garden." *Progressive Architecture*, December 1961, 136–141.

"Row Housing: Can It Help Solve the Builder's #1 Problem?" *House + Home*, July 1955. 102–117.

Schoen, Elin. "Lawrence Halprin: Humanizing the City Environment." *American Way* (American Airlines), November 1972, 13–19.

"Seattle's 'Tomorrow Park' Opens July 4: It's Built on Top of a Freeway." *Sunset*, July 1976, 52–55.

"Second Home Communities: The Sea Ranch." *Architectural Record*, November 1965, 152–55.

Sorkin, Michael. "Bunker Hill Mentality." *Arts + Architecture*, Fall 1981, 45–47.

Spencer, Robert. "Creative Forum: 30 Distinguished Americans Speak Out." *Creative Living* (Northwestern Mutual Life), Winter 1976, 21.

_____. "Ghirardelli Square: The Square That Isn't a Square." *American Way* (American Airlines), November 1972, 20–23.

Stewart, Elizabeth. "The Halprins." *Pacific Sun*, February 1981, 3.

Temko, Allan. "The Flowering of San Francisco." *Horizon*, January 1959, 4–24.

_____. "'Planned Chaos' on the Piazza." *Architectural Forum*, October 1961, 112–17.

"These Hospitals are Architecture." *Architectural Forum*, September 1959, 150–57.

"U.S. Designs for Hospitals Abroad." *Progressive Architecture*, February 1961, 122–131.

Von Eckhardt, Wolf. "A Beautiful Plaza, Designed for Fun." *Smithsonian*, November 1970, 52–56.

_____. "The Movers and the Makers." *Venture*, October–November 1967, 130–140.

_____. "A Rose Garden Honoring Roosevelt." *The Washington Post*, July 5, 1975.

"What Makes This House So Good?" *House + Home*, April 1953, 110–13.

Woodbridge, Sally. "Green Lid for 1–5." *Progressive Architecture*, June 1977, 86–87.

Zevi, Bruno, ed. "Consultazione Internazionale per La Fabbrica Fiat Lingotto: Progetti di Architetti e Gruppi di Architetti, Lawrence Halprin." *L'Architettura*, Maggio, 1984, 336–37.

Films

Halprin, Lawrence. *Designing Environments for Everyone*. Produced by Michael Lerner for the Landscape Architecture Foundation, 1984.

_____, with Anna Halprin. *How Sweet It Is*. RoundHouse, 1976. (A film about dance, theater in the environment.)

_____, produced by Sue Yung Li Ikeda, for RoundHouse. *Le Pink Grapefruit*. Phoenix Films, 1976. (A film about the environment and art of Salvador Dali; received Special Jury Award, San Francisco Film Festival, 1976.)

Fleck, Glen. *The Franklin Delano Roosevelt Memorial*. In collaboration with Sue Yung Li Ikeda and Lawrence Halprin for RoundHouse, 1978.

Pidgeon, Monica. *The Ecology of Form*. Pidgeon Audio Visual, 1982. (A slide show with sound about Halprin.)

Sources of Illustrations